100
COMMON WILDFLOWERS
OF CENTRAL CALIFORNIA

D1565847

Susan Lamb

WESTERN NATIONAL PARKS ASSOCIATION
TUCSON, ARIZONA

ACKNOWLEDGMENTS

Thanks to Keith Warner, OFM, of the Environmental Studies faculty at Santa Clara University and to botanist Jim Lockwood, OFM, for their expertise, inspiration, and companionship. Also thanks to Sharon Franklet for her help with the ethnobotany, to George Butterworth and Denis Kearns for their knowledge of plants in the southern range of this book, and to editor Steve Phillips for his attention to detail and for his patient guidance of this project.

Lamb, Susan, 1951-
      100 common wildflowers of central California / by Susan Lamb.—1st ed.
          p. cm.
      Includes bibliographical references and index.
      ISBN 1-58369-068-9 (pbk.)
      1. Wild flowers—California—Identification. 2. Wild
      flowers—California—Pictorial works. I. Title: One hundred wildflowers
      of central California.
      II. Title.
QK149.L36 2005
582.13'09794—dc22

                                      2005022789

The net proceeds from WNPA publications support educational and research programs in the national parks. Receive a free Western National Parks Association catalog, featuring hundreds of publications. Email: info@wnpa.org or visit www.wnpa.org

ISBN-10 1-58369-068-9
ISBN-13 978-1-58369-068-0

Edited by Steve Phillips
Designed by Nancy Campana/Campana Design
Cover Photograph Larry Ulrich
Illustrations Karolyn Darrow
Map Design Deborah Reade
Printing C&C Offset
Printed in China

Pitcher Sage

Wildflowers are ambassadors from nature. Their loveliness and simplicity beckon us closer, drawing us into a realm of sunlight and promise.

But wildflowers don't bloom just for people, of course. Strictly speaking, the purpose of a flower is to produce seeds that will ensure the future survival of its species. Flowers do this by packaging their genetic material—their DNA—in grains of pollen that are produced by their *anthers,* or male parts (see diagram on the following page). Pollinators—insects, birds, bats, and even the wind—carry this pollen to the *stigmas,* one of the female parts, of flowers of the same species. The pollen combines with the DNA of that flower's *ovules* to develop into a viable seed.

Over time, different flowers have developed specific shapes, colors, fragrances, nectars, and blooming schedules in order to attract specific pollinators. Pollinators have also evolved physical characteristics and behaviors in response to the shapes and habits of the available flowers. These close partnerships make it more likely that the pollinator will deliver the pollen to another flower of the same species.

The great diversity of wildflowers in central California matches an enormous diversity in insects. In the mere twenty-five square miles of Pinnacles National Monument, for example, there are 389 species of native bees ranging from tiny mosquito-sized bees to huge bees the size of a human thumb. When other pollinators are considered—beetles, crane flies, gnats, butterflies, moths, hummingbirds, and so on—it becomes evident that the world of wildflowers and their pollinators must be very rich indeed.

Plant-pollinator partnerships go beyond the brief period when flowers are in bloom. The leaves of *host* plants provide food and cover for caterpillars, which will later metamorphose into pollinating butterflies. In some cases, the caterpillars ingest toxins that they *sequester,* or store through ensuing developmental phases, so that the butterflies they will become are unpalatable to predators. Butterflies also imbibe chemicals in the nectar of certain flowers, which they use to produce *pheromones*—hormones that attract potential mates. For these butterflies, finding their specific nectar plants is essential to their success.

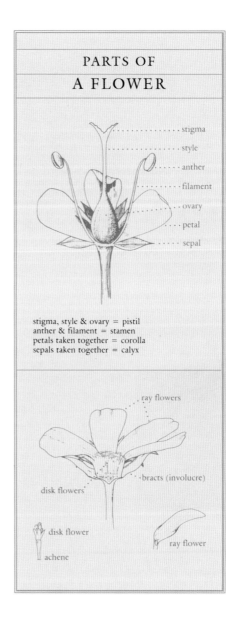

PARTS OF
A FLOWER

stigma
style
anther
filament
ovary
petal
sepal

stigma, style & ovary = pistil
anther & filament = stamen
petals taken together = corolla
sepals taken together = calyx

ray flowers

bracts (involucre)

disk flowers

disk flower

ray flower

achene

THE CLIMATE OF CENTRAL CALIFORNIA

Wildflowers are surprisingly informative historians. Columbines and other flowers tell us that as the last ice age ended, many plants in central California adapted to the increasing warmth, dryness, and change in pollinators. Evening primroses and other plants advanced from the south and mingled with them. Some diversified into new genera such as *Clarkias*. The resulting plant communities still reflect their mixed origins.

Shooting Star

Common Monkeyflower

One way or another, central California's wildflowers adapted to a Mediterranean-type climate of mild, moist winters and six or seven months of hot, dry weather. To survive without rain from April to November, most central California plants have various combinations of thick skins, surface hairs, resins, and small or upright leaves in order to reduce evaporation.

They are also adapted to the conditions of specific niches within this climate regime. Common monkeyflowers shelter in moist and shady riparian areas, while California poppies thrive in dry, sunny grasslands.

Timing is critical. Ephemeral annuals carry out their life cycles during favorable weeks and spend the rest of the year as seeds. Certain shrubs drop their leaves in summer, becoming *summer dormant*. Some plants simply do not emerge or bloom in years when conditions aren't right. An extreme example of this occurred after the late spring rains of 2005, when the rare Mount Diablo buckwheat blossomed. The flower had not been seen since 1936.

When the rains begin—usually in November—the roots of perennial plants and the seeds of annuals absorb moisture and soon begin to grow. Many spend winter as rosettes of leaves hugging the ground and soaking up sunlight, preparing to flower when their pollinators need them and vice versa. Some, like tooth wort, bloom early in the year in response to the rains, while jimson weed and others store moisture in tubers or succulent leaves for when they blossom later.

Tooth Wort

Keir Morse

Whispering Bells

Distinct communities of plants have developed in response to the variations in rainfall, temperature, slope, and soil that are found at different elevations in central California. Generally, the air is drier and temperatures are warmer in the interior and toward the southern part of the region. These are known as *bioregions*. Within each bioregion, south- and west-facing slopes receive more sun and are warmer and drier than north- or east-facing hillsides.

California is also a geologic patchwork where the soils vary considerably in fertility, porosity, and chemical makeup. There are sandy soils, rich soils, clay, and challenging areas of serpentine soils that have developed from metamorphic rocks. These serpentine soils are high in magnesium and heavy metals, tend to be pH neutral or alkaline, and are lacking in essential plant nutrients, and yet plants like pitcher sage thrive in them. "Adobe," which is common in California, is a form of clayey soil largely made up of small, flat mineral particles. These particles pack together when wet, blocking the growth of roots, slowing drainage, and preventing oxygen from reaching the roots. Only certain plants, such as Ithuriel's spear, can flourish in adobe soils.

Plant and animal partnerships also influence what grows where. In some places, for instance, burrowing ground squirrels aerate the soil, fertilize it, increase its capacity to hold water, and scatter seeds through it.

Owl's-clover

GRASSLAND

The floors of central California's valleys are mostly semiarid grasslands originally composed of deep-rooted perennial bunchgrasses that resprout after fire, along with riparian and marshy areas. Where the original grassland is intact, spring brings carpets of California poppies, miniature lupine, buttercups, and owl's-clover. Depressions called *vernal pools* that are filled with winter rainfall dry out as summer approaches, their retreating shorelines frothing with meadowfoam and goldfields. Saltbush and salt-tolerant annuals such as tidytips flourish in low-lying flats with alkaline soil.

Grassland once covered more than a fourth of California, but undisturbed stretches of it are rare today. The Central Valley has been widely cultivated, the water table lowered, and alien plants introduced. Brome and other exotic annual grasses have disrupted the natural cycle of fire, burning very hot early in the season with devastating effects on the native flora. The result of these changes has been a loss of wildlife habitat; the pronghorn and elk that once browsed the bunchgrasses here are gone. The diversity of plants is declining, but there are still precious pockets of grassland where the native flora persists.

RIPARIAN

Seasonal and permanent streams trickle down ravines in central California's foothills and across its valley bottoms, creating riparian areas. These offer a lifeline for moisture-dependent plants, especially hoary nettle and other perennials. Cattails, ferns, and duckweed flourish here; sycamore, willow, and cottonwood keep their roots moist in and along these streams as well.

Wildlife frequents riparian areas, particularly at dawn and dusk. Western Mono, Miwuk, and other Native Californians have long collected sedges, rushes, and ferns here to make baskets and cordage as well as the fiddle-heads of chain ferns for food and bracken ferns to tan leather.

Even when streambeds appear dry, water may persist a foot or two below their surface. Water-dependent plants indicate where this is the case. Where a riparian area is only seasonal or the water table is very deep during the dry season, the leaves of ferns and other plants—including California buckeye trees—shrivel or drop off as the plants become summer dormant.

WOODLANDS

Grassy foothills rise above the valleys, too dry to support dense forests but dotted with valley oak, coast live oak, and Engelmann oak, especially on their north-facing slopes, in canyons, and along streams. California buckeye and gray pine occur on these foothills as well.

Oak woodlands sustain both annual and perennial grasses and forbs. In spring, the foothills come alive with plantain and colorful patches of Chinese houses. Oaks are aerial habitats in themselves, sustaining an astonishing array of wildlife by providing acorns and leaves as food and by offering sheltered hollows, perches, nesting sites, and travel corridors.

The more arid conditions found in the interior and toward the southern reaches of central California favor juniper woodland. Junipers are extremely hardy trees; one *Juniperus californica* above the Carrizo Plain has been determined to be 990 years old!

CHAPARRAL

Chaparral dominates the drier hillsides. It is a community characterized by drought-adapted shrubs such as chamise, buck brush, mountain mahogany, and toyon. Chaparral adaptations include shrubby stature; small, thick-skinned, resinous, hairy, or waxy leaves; substantial root systems; and summer dormancy. Manzanita can change the angle of its leaves to minimize their exposure to the sun.

Many chaparral shrubs are in the rose family, and most produce berries or seeds that are eaten by birds, squirrels, and gray foxes. These shrubs take advantage of being eaten. The seeds of holly-leaved cherry, for instance, must be softened and then distributed via the digestive systems of animals in order to germinate and recolonize burned areas.

Chaparral plants are well adapted to fire, which normally occurs every five to twenty years. They cope with fire in different ways. Chamise and certain other shrubs resprout from root crowns. *Fire followers,* on the other hand, are often short-lived species with a "bank" of seeds in the soil that germinate in response to heat or smoke. These plants thrive in the open spaces created by fire until other plants grow up and out-compete them for light and nutrients.

Depending upon local conditions, different chaparral shrubs may predominate. Chamise is typical of the dry-phase chaparral on south-facing slopes. Holly-leaf cherry, manzanita, scrub oak, and toyon prevail in the moist-phase chaparral of north-facing hillsides.

ROCK AND SCREE

Some slopes have so little soil that they are classified as rock and *scree* (rocky debris). They endure extremes of temperature from cold nights to sun-baked days. Bitter root, fringed onion, and other graceful scree wildflowers persist in this hostile environment by hoarding moisture in their tubers and bulbs, while *Dudleyas* store it in succulent leaves.

COMMUNITY RELATIONS

There is much more happening in these plant communities than meets the eye. Soil teems with bacteria, nematodes, and microscopic insects that improve its texture and add to its fertility. Mushrooms get our attention, but they are only the aboveground fruits of a mass of threadlike *mycorrhizae* in the soil. Mycorrhizae take nutrients from the roots of surrounding plants, but they also help those plants to absorb water and minerals in a *symbiotic* (mutually beneficial) relationship.

There are strictly *parasitic* relationships in these communities, too. Oak mistletoe and California dodder penetrate other plants with *haustoria*, or probes, in order to tap their nutrients. Oak mistletoe grows as an olive-green clump on the young branches of oak trees and is especially obvious in winter when the trees look otherwise lifeless. California dodder is a slender, leafless, flowering vine that twines over other plants in an orange tangle. Both parasites stress but seldom kill their hosts.

Wildflower seeds use various partners to help them disperse. Some seeds are encased in tasty fruits to be softened and transported in the digestive tracts of animals. Seeds with grasping claws can attach to passing fur. Ants collect many different kinds of seeds that come complete with *elaiosomes*—fatty appendages—and carry them back to their nests for food, effectively dispersing and planting them.

Our understanding of plant chemistry has increased greatly over the past twenty-five years. We now understand that sunlight prompts plants to produce chemicals called *phytochromes*. When enough of these chemicals have accumulated, they trigger certain functions in the plant. Phytochromes are partly why plants are able to coordinate their activities with those of their pollinators.

Larry Ulrich

Fiddleneck in the Temblor Range

The flowers of central California choose their moments carefully. They vary the amount and quality of the pollen and nectar they produce at different times of the day, depending upon who will be in the neighborhood. Some bloom at night to attract moths; others waft their fragrances into the air only when conditions allow a certain butterfly to be on the wing.

Plants can tolerate a certain amount of nibbling but must protect themselves from being completely consumed. To defend themselves, many produce toxins, which often have a bitter taste. Some pollinators and their young have adapted to these chemicals. Milkweed, to use a familiar example, produces pyrazine alkaloids that are ingested by monarch caterpillars and remain present in the adult butterflies. Predators are conditioned not to eat these brightly colored, toxic butterflies; they leave them alone to pollinate flowers. These pollinators then use the minerals and plant chemicals

Pinnacles National Monument

they consume to produce their own chemicals for defense and courtship.

Indigenous central Californians—Ohlone, Salinan, Miwok, Yokuts, Kitanemuk, Tataviam, and Chumash—have understood many properties of the local plants for millennia. They continue to use central California's flowering plants for food, dye, seasoning, fiber, soap, and medicine. Spanish missionaries incorporated California flora into their herbal apothecaries, and many native plants also entered the U.S. Pharmacopeia (USP) during the nineteenth and early twentieth centuries. But plant-people interactions are not always positive—the line between a medicine and a poison can be very thin.

Research continues to reveal remarkable strategies that plants have developed for the survival of their species as well as benefits to others. Yet there will always be more to the world of wildflowers than we can possibly imagine.

ABOUT THIS BOOK

The wildflowers represented in this guide are native to the sunny interior valleys of California and to the grassy, oak-studded foothills that surround them. Many of these flowers are also found in California's coastal areas, mountains, or deserts. This book will be helpful in identifying wildflowers that are likely to bloom from Paso Robles to Pinnacles National Monument, and from Carrizo Plain National Monument to the western gates of Yosemite National Park. County, state, and national parks are good places to seek out wildflowers. There are also several "hotlines" that describe which flowers are blooming and where they may be seen in the state. These hotlines are updated throughout the year and may be found on-line by searching for "California wildflower hotlines."

The distribution of the wildflowers in this book may be found in the appendix. Common and scientific names, as well as the distribution and blooming dates, of the wildflowers in this book are based on the *Manual of Flowering Plants of California* by Willis Linn Jepson (1867–1946). Jepson was professor of botany at the University of California from 1899 until 1937, and an avid hiker and conservationist. He founded the California Botanical Society and was a charter member of the Save-the-Redwoods League and the Sierra Club.

Jepson's *Manual of Flowering Plants of California* is now the responsibility of the Jepson Flora Project at the Jepson Herbarium, University of California. The manual is continuously expanded, refined, and updated. It is available on-line at http://ucjeps.berkeley.edu/jepson_flora_project.html.

POISON
OAK

Anyone on a wildflower quest in central California should know how to recognize and avoid *Toxicodendron diversilobum,* or poison oak. Poison oak gets its name from the lobed shape of its leaves, which resemble those of a valley oak tree (the two are not related). It grows as a shrub in the chaparral and often as a climbing vine in riparian areas.

Poison oak is a widespread hazard. The sap contains *urushiol,* a toxic substance that causes a rash on human skin. Unlike the immediate irritation caused by contact with hoary nettle, a poison oak rash takes

hours or days to develop. It begins as a red, itchy patch on the skin, progresses to localized swelling and oozing blisters, and usually takes ten days or so to run its course. The affliction can be quite severe. Firefighters and other outdoor workers who contract serious cases of poison oak are eligible for disability payments from the state of California.

It is estimated that seven out of ten people are sensitive to poison oak and can contract the rash by brushing against any part of the plant. Indigenous Californians, however, sometimes wove the young stems of poison oak into baskets—the Pomo even dyed their baskets with poison oak sap. Some of them may have been immune to the toxin, whereas others must have taken great care in working with the plant. They also made a number of salves and poultices from other local plants to soothe the rash when it did occur.

Deer, cattle, horses, and birds eat poison oak leaves and fruits with no ill effects, and packrats build nests of its stems. The evolutionary purpose of poison oak's rash-causing sap is still not clear to botanists.

1 · White Globe Lily, Fairy Lantern

Fragile and luminous, globe lilies gleam from shaded niches in open woods or brush. Only large or long-tongued bees, such as bumblebees, can access their dangling flowers of three overlapping petals, which protect their pollen from rain and wind. Their slender leaves with parallel veins resemble grass. (*Calochortus* is Greek for "beautiful grass.")

Janet Horton

The genus *Calochortus* originated in the Coast Ranges of California and diversified into dozens of species and four basic shapes: mariposa and star tulips with spread-open petals, cat's ears with smaller *trichomotous* (hairy) petals, and egg-shaped globe lilies. Globe lilies are *endemic* (restricted) to the southern two-thirds of California.

SCIENTIFIC NAME	*Calochortus albus*
FAMILY	**Liliaceae** Lily
BLOOM	April–June

2 · Tooth Wort, Milkmaids

Larry Ulrich

Tooth wort overwinters as a rosette of leaves. It is one of the first flowers to bloom in moist areas and shady places such as woods and canyons. Small bees, small flies, and butterflies are its pollinators. It hosts several species of white butterflies.

Some *Cardamine* have medicinal qualities, but Tooth wort has nothing to do with the treatment of teeth. Its name comes from a toothlike projection at the base of its petals.

Flowers of the mustard family have four petals that bend back in the form of a cross. Edible Brassicacea include brussels sprouts, cabbage, broccoli, cauliflower, horseradish, and radishes. Some Brassicacea are eaten as salads and greens, though they contain oil that can irritate skin and a peppery sap that may require lengthy cooking and rinsing to render palatable.

SCIENTIFIC NAME	*Cardamine californica* var. *californica*
FAMILY	**Brassicaceae** Mustard
BLOOM	February–May

3 · Narrow-leaved Fringepod, Lacepod

Charles Rettner

SCIENTIFIC NAME	*Thysanocarpus laciniatus*
FAMILY	**Brassicaceae** Mustard
BLOOM	March–May

Fringepod is a very common annual found in grasslands, shaded sites, and rocky ridges. Its minute, four-petaled flowers usually escape notice until their oval seedpods form. Thin sections along the edges of these flat pods look like tiny notches, making the pods appear fringed; Greek *thysan* means "fringe" and *carpus* is "pod" or "fruit." *Laciniatus* means "narrow leaves" in Latin.

Like all mustards, fringepods bloom progressively up their stems, leaving behind pods that dry out and split to release their seeds. Unlike most mustards, these pods have only one chamber. The condiment mustard is ground from the seeds of European Brassicacea.

4 · Jewelflower

Keir Morse

A jewelflower is a miniature purplish-white blossom that is all but hidden inside a large, purple *calyx*. The calyx is the outer layer of a flower that protects its vital and delicate parts—anthers, stigma, nectaries, petals—during their development. In most flowers, the calyx splits open or drops away to expose these parts, but the jewelflower's unusual calyx of three fused *sepals*, or modified leaves (with a fourth spread out below), stays in place and is showier than its petals. It looks like a ruby on a long, spindly stem.

Jewelflowers are found in chaparral, dry grasslands, and open woodlands. Several *Streptanthus* species occur on serpentine soils. They are host plants for the caterpillars of Sara orange-tip butterflies.

SCIENTIFIC NAME	*Streptanthus glandulosus* ssp. *glandulosus*
FAMILY	**Brassicaceae** Mustard
BLOOM	April–May

5 · Evening Snow

Evening snow wafts its sweet scent into the cool night air to attract hawkmoths, then closes each morning. Its calyx is a cylinder that encloses the lower ends of its five petals, which are fused into a funnel.

This shape admits only long-tongued pollinators.

Linanthus comes from the Greek *linon*, "flax", and *anthos*, "flower," but despite its resemblance to flax, evening snow belongs to an entirely different family. *Linanthus* is primarily a California genus, with about forty species endemic to the state. *Linanthus dichotomus*, however, is found in Nevada, Utah, and Arizona as well as in California. It blooms in open areas as they dry out from winter moisture, especially those with serpentine soils. An annual that produces many seeds, it favors grassy, gravelly, or sandy places.

SCIENTIFIC NAME	*Linanthus dichotomus*
FAMILY	**Polemoniaceae** Phlox
BLOOM	April–June

6 · Miner's Lettuce

The flowers of miner's lettuce are only 1/8 to 1/4 inch wide. They bloom on stems that grow through the plant's round upper leaf (which is actually two leaves grown together). The plant does not generally grow erect, but rather sprawls up to fifteen inches in width. Miner's lettuce requires plenty of moisture; it prefers riparian areas and sometimes grows in streams. The primary pollinators are animals: Mourning doves, juncos, and horned larks eat the seeds, while kangaroo rats consume both the seeds and the leaves. Indigenous people of California eat the leaves of miner's lettuce raw or cooked, and brew them

SCIENTIFIC NAME	*Claytonia perfoliata*
FAMILY	**Portulacaceae** Purslane
BLOOM	February–May

for a laxative tea. Settlers have followed their example, especially during the nineteenth century in an effort to avoid scurvy.

7 · California Saxifrage

Charles Rettner

The five-petaled, dime-sized flowers of California saxifrage bloom in riparian areas and shaded woodlands. Saxifrage appears to be sprinkled with red dots, which on closer inspection prove to be its ten *anthers,* or pollen-bearing parts.

The genus *Saxifraga* takes its name from Latin *saxum,* "rock," and *frangere* "to break." It is assumed that this name comes from the tendency for plants of this genus to grow in rock crevices, but an alternate explanation is that some herbalists once used preparations of saxifrage to break kidney stones.

SCIENTIFIC NAME	*Saxifraga californica*
FAMILY	**Saxifragaceae** Saxifrage
BLOOM	February–June

8 · Stinging Phacelia

Stinging phacelia is an annual plant found in coarse soils of moist chaparral and coniferous forests. It produces caterpillar-like coils of small, five-petaled, wide-open flowers that provide nectar to a range of pollinators, including wasps, flies, bee flies, ants, and honeybees. Hikers dodge this plant to avoid the rash that comes from contact with its stiff yellow hairs. These hairs are highly irritating due to a compound produced by the glands at its base. *Phacelia* is from the Greek *phakelos,* "cluster," for its one-sided clusters of flowers. *Phacelia malvifo-lia*'s leaves are similar to leaves in Malvaceae, the mallow family. Its flowers open in the morning, withering with the afternoon heat. *Mentzelia* sprawls or reclines to form mats or clumps. The oily seeds of some species can be parched or roasted and eaten.

Keir Morse

SCIENTIFIC NAME	*Phacelia malvifolia*
FAMILY	**Hydrophyllaceae** Waterleaf
BLOOM	April–July

9 · Popcornflower

Popcornflowers are common in grasslands and woodlands. Their stem tips are initially coiled and unwind as they mature. They are lined with flower buds that open into tubular, five-lobed corollas. Popcornflower roots, stems, and leaves contain a purple dye.

Visiting bees and monarch butterflies imbibe toxic alkaloids as well as nectar from Boraginaceae. These toxins protect them from birds and are used by male butterflies to make *pheromones*, which are chemicals that attract female butterflies.

Charles Rettner

SCIENTIFIC NAME	*Plagiobothrys nothofulvus*
FAMILY	**Boraginaceae** Borage
BLOOM	March–May

10 · Heliotrope

Wild heliotrope is a common grassland and riparian flower that blooms in alkaline or saline sand or clay, especially around vernal pools. It develops from a perennial root. This wild heliotrope is not related to the garden ornamental, and it is also sometimes confused with some of the white species of *Phacelia*. It is a popular butterfly nectar plant.

The genus *Heliotropium* takes its name from the Greek words *helio*, "sun," and *tropium*, "turning," because several members bloom near the summer solstice when the rising sun reverses its progress along the horizon.

Larry Ulrich

SCIENTIFIC NAME	*Heliotropium currasavicum*
FAMILY	**Boraginaceae** Borage
BLOOM	March–October

11 · California Man-root, Wild Cucumber

Charles Rettner

SCIENTIFIC NAME	*Marah fabaceus*
FAMILY	**Cucurbitaceae** Gourd
BLOOM	February–April

Man-root is a sprawling vine that is found in the chaparral and along streams and washes. It has a huge, branching root that enables it to regrow quickly after dying back during the dry months.

Marah fabaceus has separate male and female flowers that look much alike, both consisting of five petals fused into a star-shaped cup. The pollen-producing flowers cluster on short stems, while solitary female flowers emerge at branching points. Around dawn, heavy native bees search from blossom to blossom for pollen and nectar, inadvertently fertilizing the female flowers.

The Cucurbitaceae include squash, cucumbers, and melons, but some members contain *cucubitacin* toxins that beetles store as a defense. Man-root is bitter and can be toxic. Its spiny fruits have beanlike seeds, hence its Latin epithet *M. fabaceus*, "beanlike."

12 · Jimson Weed, Thorn-apple

Jimson weed is a large-leaved, night-blooming plant that emerges in moist, coarse soils from a perennial tuber. Its slightly toothed, funnel-shaped flowers with their musty scent attract large hawkmoths in the evenings.

Jimson weed produces a prickly round fruit, but no part of the plant is edible. It contains tropane alkaloids that have effects ranging from hallucinations to death. Hawkmoths retain these alkaloids as a defense against predators.

The common name Jimson comes from James-town, Virginia, where a similar species of *Datura* is found. The Solanaceae family includes bell peppers, tomatoes, potatoes, eggplant, tobacco, and petunias.

Larry Ulrich

SCIENTIFIC NAME	*Datura wrightii*
FAMILY	**Solanaceae** Nightshade
BLOOM	April–October

13 · Silver Puffs

Silver puffs resemble dandelions, but they have pointed green bracts that extend past their yellow rays. Their common name refers to their conspicuous spherical seed heads, which are composed of five-pointed silver stars. They bloom in  dry grasslands, chaparral, deserts, and blue oak woodlands, generally in loose soils.

Silver puffs are common annual flowers whose strategy is to produce many seeds that are attached to "parachutes" of hairs arranged in crowns like umbrellas. Winds carry these seeds over a wide area, enabling silver puff seeds to reach any habitat that might meet their requirements for germination and growth.

SCIENTIFIC NAME	*Uropappus lindleyi*
FAMILY	**Asteraceae** Sunflower
BLOOM	April–May

14 · Blow-wives

Blow-wives are inconspicuous when in bloom. Their flower heads do not open wide and they lack the long, showy ray flowers of most other members of their family. Extended green sepals all but conceal their yellow disk flowers.

Like silver puffs, blow-wives attract more attention for their seed heads. These are made up of dense five- to eight-pointed stars in globelike clusters. The rays of these "stars" look like silver ribbons. When ripe, the plumed seeds detach easily and are carried aloft by the slightest breeze. Blow-wives are common in sunny grasslands, including those on serpentine soils.

SCIENTIFIC NAME	*Achyrachaena mollis*
FAMILY	**Asteraceae** Sunflower
BLOOM	April–May

15 · Wild Buckwheat

Keir Morse

Long-stemmed buckwheat is a common perennial shrub in dry places such as chaparral. Like other members of its family, it has tiny flowers composed of sepals without any petals, arranged in balls that are widely separated along its upper stems.

Many different pollinators, including bees and flies, visit members of the genus *Eriogonum* throughout the day. Relying on a range of different pollinators is insurance against a drop in the population of any particular insect. Long-stemmed buckwheat is the host plant for gorgon copper, Acmon blue, and dotted blue butterflies.

California has many forbs and shrubs in the buckwheat family, usually found in open, rocky areas. Buckwheat seeds are food for many animals, including humans.

SCIENTIFIC NAME	*Eriogonum elongatum*
FAMILY	**Polygonaceae** Buckwheat
BLOOM	August–November

16 · California Buckwheat

California buckwheat has small white flowers in compound *umbels* (flat-topped flower clusters) that turn reddish as they age. These flowers attract countless pollinators. The plant is host to Acmon blue, lupine blue, Bernardino dotted blue, and Mormon metalmark caterpillars, and its flowers are an important source of nectar for butterflies. It is an important shrub for the production of honey in California. (Honeybees are not native to North America; they apparently arrived with English colonists in Virginia in 1622.) California buckwheat seeds attract ants, which carry them underground, where they later sprout. Like other chaparral shrubs, California buckwheat thrives in burned-over areas, becoming more abundant after natural disturbances such as fire or flooding.

Keir Morse

SCIENTIFIC NAME	*Eriogonum fasciculatum* var. *foliolosum*
FAMILY	**Polygonaceae** Buckwheat
BLOOM	March–October

17 · Buck Brush

When in bloom, buck brush looks like clouds caught on the hillsides. Its small flowers form in dense clusters that are usually white but occasionally have a blue tinge like glacial ice. Their intense fragrance has led to their nickname of California lilac. This shrub dominates certain areas of chaparral and is common on rocky slopes and ridges in dry soils including sand and serpentine.

Keir Morse

Buck brush is browsed by deer. It hosts several hairstreak butterflies as well as California tortoiseshell butterflies. Ceanothus stem gall moths lay eggs on its flower buds; their larvae bore into its stems and cause galls that are used as rattles by indigenous Californians. The seedpods burst in summer, shooting their contents away from the mother plant.

SCIENTIFIC NAME	*Ceanothus cuneatus* var. *cuneatus*
FAMILY	**Rhamnaceae** Buckthorn
BLOOM	March–May

18 · Chamise

Chamise, or greasewood, is a key chaparral species. Its needlelike leaves contain volatile substances that ignite readily, as does a resinous material in its bark. Chamise also develops dead wood as the years go by. All of these characteristics make it prone to burning, but it resprouts quickly from its root crown after fires.

Charles Rettner

Like many chaparral shrubs, chamise is in the rose family. Its small flowers have five petals and bloom in spikes. It is popular with bees. Chamise is also the host plant for spring azure butterflies, whose caterpillars eat only the flowers. California natives use chamise tea as a remedy for colds and cramps.

SCIENTIFIC NAME	*Adenostoma fasciculatum*
FAMILY	**Rosaceae** Rose
BLOOM	May–June

19 · Narrow-leaf Milkweed

Keir Morse

Narrow-leaf milkweed is a perennial plant common to dry ground in the foothills and valleys of interior California. Its clustered flowers are strange, five-pointed stars that have fleshy sepals and white petals. Milkweed seeds are attached to parachutes that burst by the hundreds from pods in the fall.

Milkweeds are perhaps best known as the host plants for monarch butterflies. They contain asclepin, a heart poison with a bitter taste that monarch caterpillars consume and store in their tissues to deter predators. The caterpillars cut the leaf veins of asclepias before feeding, to avoid ingesting the latex in its milky juice. Indigenous Californians make chewing gum of this juice and use the plant's fibers for cordage.

SCIENTIFIC NAME	*Asclepias fascicularis*
FAMILY	**Asclepiadaceae** Milkweed
BLOOM	June–July

20 · Fremont's Death Camas

Fremont's death camas grows on grassy or wooded slopes or chaparral wherever the soil is deep enough to accommodate their bulbs, which can be as wide as three inches. Also known as star lilies, they have six-pointed, ivory-colored flowers in clusters at the ends of their stems.

Fremont's death camas contains the alkaloid zygadenine, which is toxic to animals and humans (although animals instinctively avoid it). It was named for John Charles Fremont (1813–1890), an army officer who collected plants on four journeys of exploration in the western United States.

Charles Rettner

SCIENTIFIC NAME	*Zigadenus fremontii*
FAMILY	**Liliaceae** Lily
BLOOM	May–July

21 · Soap Plant, Amole

Soap plant blooms in the evening or on cloudy days (the specific name *pomeridianum* means "of the afternoon"). Its strong fragrance and back-curved white sepals and petals attract night-flying moths. Soap plant hosts the caterpillars of its pollinating moths as well as of the brown elfin butterfly. It blossoms on plains and hills, in open brush, and in woods.

The bulbs of this plant may be crushed to use as soap or strewn on stream waters to stun fish. The bulbs are also roasted and pulped for use as glue and as a salve for poison oak. Fibers of its grasslike, wavy-edged leaves are woven into baskets and used as brushes.

Charles Rettner

SCIENTIFIC NAME	*Chlorogalum pomeridianum* var. *pomeridianum*
FAMILY	**Liliaceae** Lily
BLOOM	May–August

22 · Black Sage

Black sage is an important bee plant—*mellifera* means "honey-bearing." It has typical mint family flowers in which two petals are fused into an upper lip and three petals combine to form a lower, pouting lip—in this case twice as long as the upper—above a tubular corolla. The flowers occur in widely spaced clusters along a spikelike stem. Black sage is found in coastal sage scrub and in chaparral at lower elevations. It flourishes in burned-over areas.

Salvia is from Latin *salvia*–"to heal." Mediterranean members of Lamiaceae include basil, oregano, marjoram, thyme, catnip, lavender, and sage.

Keir Morse

SCIENTIFIC NAME	*Salvia mellifera*
FAMILY	**Lamiaceae** Mint
BLOOM	April–July

23 · Everlasting, Cudweed

Charles Rettner

SCIENTIFIC NAME	*Gnaphalium canescens* ssp. *beneolens*
FAMILY	**Asteraceae** Sunflower
BLOOM	July–November

Everlasting is a study in flower anatomy. It is true to the name of its genus, which comes from the Greek *gnaphalon*, "a lock of wool." Its flowers are in fuzzy terminal *glomerules* (clusters) clasped by *bracts* (modified leaves associated with a flower cluster), with bases that look like snips of fleece. It's a fuzzy plant in general, its slender leaves covered with short hairs. This hairiness protects it from drying out in its arid environment.

Everlasting shoots up to almost three feet from a perennial root. It blooms on open slopes from summer through fall—everlasting indeed compared with most other central California flowers. It is a host plant to American lady butterflies.

24 · California Goosefoot, Pigweed

SCIENTIFIC NAME	*Chenopodium californicum*
FAMILY	**Chenopodiaceae** Goosefoot
BLOOM	March–June

Goosefoot produces small, greenish-white flowers clustered around a spike that emerges from a perennial, carrotlike root. Its leaves are wavy edged and slightly toothed. It favors streambeds and moist slopes with sandy or clay soils on open foothills.

Although considered a noxious weed by modern commercial farmers, pigweed has long been an important food and medicinal plant of the Americas. Wild species are consumed as raw or cooked greens, both as nourishment and to treat stomachaches. Native Californians use goosefoot-leaf poultices to reduce swelling and soothe aching teeth, and they brew it as a wash for rheumatism. Goosefoot seeds are used in baking and porridge, and the root is grated for soap.

Keir Morse

California plantain is a common annual in woodlands, on hillsides, and in grassy flats. It thrives in sandy, clayey, or serpentine soils. California plantain flowers are ethereal—each with four membranous petals, protruding stamens, and diaphanous filaments—arranged around the tip of a stalk.

California plantain is a host plant of the common buckeye butterfly. It has green leaves that are edible by humans, although they contain iridoid toxins that are *sequestered* (stored) by caterpillars to deter predators. The seeds have a mucilaginous coating that enables them to absorb and retain water. Indigenous Californians discovered early on that this property made these seeds useful as laxatives.

Keir Morse

SCIENTIFIC NAME	*Plantago erecta*
FAMILY	**Plantaginaceae** Plantain
BLOOM	March–May

26 · Desert Candle

The small, simple white flowers of desert candle have purplish-tipped sepals when in bud and their petals have purplish veins. They bloom on short stems along an unusual stout, hollow stalk that may be a foot or two tall and has oblong leaves at its base. This stalk tastes much like cabbage—which is in the same family—and is sometimes eaten boiled with meat.

Desert candle favors open, sandy or gravelly soils or rocky slopes. It is a desert annual that blooms profusely in years of adequate rainfall, often along roads where runoff increases the amount of available moisture.

SCIENTIFIC NAME	*Caulanthus inflatus*
FAMILY	**Brassicaceae** Mustard
BLOOM	March–May

Dave Welling

27· Douglas' Meadowfoam

Scott T. Smith / Larry Ulrich

SCIENTIFIC NAME	*Limnanthes douglasii*
FAMILY	**Limnanthaceae** False Mermaid
BLOOM	March–May

Meadowfoam is variable. Its bell-shaped flowers may have three or five petals; these may be all yellow or have yellow centers with white rims. They bloom on slender stalks and have sprawling, finely divided leaves that contribute to the plant's "frothy" appearance. Solitary bees pollinate meadowfoam as they collect its pollen and nectar. Birds and rodents consume its large, oily seeds.

The genus name *Limnanthes* comes from the Greek *limne,* "marsh," and *anthos,* "flower." Douglas' meadowfoam is associated with vernal pools, which are depressions in the ground that fill with winter rains. Vernal pools provide habitat for specialized, often-rare plants and animals that can tolerate fluctuating wet and dry conditions, full sun, and soil that is usually alkaline. As these pools dry out and shrink in the spring, meadowfoam blooms around them in ever-tightening circles.

28· Creamcups

Creamcups are little annuals that blossom in clayey or sandy grasslands. They are covered with soft hairs and have several stems, each bearing a simple, inch-wide poppy flower with six petals. Creamcups may be cream-colored, yellow, cream or yellow tinged with red, or a combination of these colors.

Clines are variations in the color or other characteristics of the same plant in different geographical areas. Clines are believed to develop in response to differences in the pollinators available in these different locations. As long as they are able to interbreed, clines with different-colored flowers are not considered separate species. Creamcups are host to the long-horned fairy moth.

Keir Morse

SCIENTIFIC NAME	*Platystemon californicus*
FAMILY	**Papaveraceae** Poppy
BLOOM	March–May

29 · Pipestems

Pipestems sprawl over other shrubs in chaparral and open woodlands, on hillsides, and in riparian areas. They tolerate both full sun and seasonal flooding. Their pale yellow flowers are made up of four sepals but no petals; their showiest features are the fluffy seed clusters that appear at summer's end. Their long seed plumes enable the wind to carry them far and wide.

Pipestems are named for their woody stems, which can be twenty feet long. Their leaves die back in the winter and sprout again in the spring. Rather than be shaded out by neighboring shrubs, pipestems simply climb over them to reach sunlight.

Larry Ulrich

SCIENTIFIC NAME	*Clematis lasiantha*
FAMILY	**Ranunculaceae** Buttercup
BLOOM	January–June

30 · Golden Eardrops

Dicentra chrysantha is one of at least twenty-five chaparral plants whose seeds germinate in response to smoke rather than to the "heat shock" of fire. Its seeds require a year in the soil before smoke exposure is effective. Smoke-triggered seeds have highly textured coatings and other adaptations that allow the smoke to enter them, either in gaseous form or mixed with rainwater. Different species vary in how much smoke they need and how much smoke they can tolerate, which may account for differences in the makeup of chaparral communities after fires.

The plant is toxic to livestock, especially when it grows abundantly after burns. It is sometimes placed in the family Fumariaceae.

Keir Morse

SCIENTIFIC NAME	*Dicentra chrysantha*
FAMILY	**Papaveraceae** Poppy
BLOOM	April–September

𝟹𝟷 · Sun Cup, Contorted Evening Primrose

Keir Morse

SCIENTIFIC NAME	*Camissonia contorta*
FAMILY	**Onagraceae** Evening Primrose
BLOOM	May–June

Sun cup is an annual plant of slopes and sandy soils in grasslands, chaparral, and piñon-juniper woodland. After the spring rains, its tiny flowers bloom in the evening with a sweet scent to attract nighttime pollinators. When fresh the flowers are yellow, later becoming reddish.

Members of Onagraceae are not true primroses. Primroses have five petals. Evening primroses, on the other hand, have four petals united with three or four sepals into a tube suited to the long tongues of moths, butterflies, and certain bees. *Camissonia contorta* is the host plant of several moths, including the only moth in North America that is listed as threatened or endangered: the Kern primrose sphinx moth.

The genus *Camissonia* was named for botanist Adelbert Ludwig von Chamisso, who visited California on the vessel *Rurik* in 1816.

𝟹𝟸 · Bush Poppy

Bush poppy is a perennial chaparral shrub that may grow three to nine feet in height. It has cup-shaped flowers with four petals and narrow, stiff (hence *rigida*), evergreen leaves that resemble those of willows. It tolerates serpentine soils.

Ants are attracted to a tiny edible growth on the seeds of bush poppies. Certain ants carry the seeds to ridgetops and discard them on the surface of the soil, while others deposit them in underground refuse tunnels. Either way, the seeds are widely dispersed to favorable sites. Bush poppies are fire adapted; their seeds germinate in response to smoke.

Dave Welling

SCIENTIFIC NAME	*Dendromecon rigida*
FAMILY	**Papaveraceae** Poppy
BLOOM	April–June

33 · California Buttercup

Janet Horton

SCIENTIFIC NAME	*Ranunculus californica*
FAMILY	**Ranunculaceae** Buttercup
BLOOM	February–May

California buttercups are early bloomers, cheerful harbingers of spring in moist areas of grass-lands, oak woodlands, and coniferous forests. The name of the genus is from Latin *rana,* "little frog," because buttercups are so often found in the sort of moist places where frogs live. *Ranunculus californica* is a perennial that becomes dormant in midsummer when conditions are dry.

The number of their petals varies, but California buttercups are recognizable by their glossy sheen and bright yellow color. They do not appear uniformly yellow to everyone, however; the ultraviolet light reflected at their centers makes them look like targets to bees. Buttercups contain a toxic alkaloid, but their acrid taste usually deters animals from eating them.

34 · Golden Yarrow

Golden yarrow is a perennial chaparral shrub. The name of its genus, *Eriophyllum,* comes from the Greek *erion,* "wool," and *phyllon,* "leaf." The woolliness of its leaves protects the plant, helping it to conserve water by reflecting the heat of the sun and deflecting desiccating breezes.

Its specific name, *confertiflorum,* means "crowded with flowers." Golden yarrow flower heads are made up of many individual, daisylike blooms grouped in compact clusters at the ends of the stems. They provide a comfortable landing platform for large-winged butterflies and are favored by painted ladies.

Keir Morse

SCIENTIFIC NAME	*Eriophyllum confertiflorum* var. *confertiflorum*
FAMILY	**Asteraceae** Sunflower
BLOOM	April–August

35 · Goldenaster

Keir Morse

Goldenaster is a perennial plant that blooms in open grasslands and oak woodlands in late summer. It is a classic, daisylike member of the family Asteraceae. Asteraceae were once known as Compositae, because their flower heads are not single flowers but instead are composed of many *florets,* or tiny flowers. What look like petals around the outside of the flower head are actually individual ray flowers, each with its own straplike corolla, or *ligule.* The round center of the flower head is really a cluster of small, tubular disc flowers arranged in a spiral that matures from the outside in. Butterflies often probe these disc flowers in sequence in a very slow pirouette.

Goldenaster is a popular plant with butterflies, especially skippers. It is the host plant of the Gabb's checkerspot butterfly.

SCIENTIFIC NAME	*Heterotheca sessiliflora* ssp. *echioides*
FAMILY	**Asteraceae** Sunflower
BLOOM	July–September

36 · Goldfields

In wet years, goldfields create a bright display on a range of poor soils, including alkaline, serpentine, and marine. They are annuals that bloom as the soggy soil dries around vernal pools. Goldfields flower heads

Keir Morse

Larry Ulrich

have a varying number of ray florets held aloft on wiry, reddish stems that are from four to sixteen inches high.

Abundant around vernal pools or wet, saline flats, goldfields may also cover open hills. Large, conspicuous populations like these are a strategy to attract pollinators across distances and keep them in the neighborhood. Small, solitary, black or gray bees that resemble little flies are the primary pollinators of goldfields.

SCIENTIFIC NAME	*Lasthenia californica*
FAMILY	**Asteraceae** Sunflower
BLOOM	February–June

37 · Common Madia

Common madia is an annual that blooms in dry, grassy places and open forest, often in large numbers. The plants can be as tall as four feet and are covered with sticky hairs. Their three-toothed ray flowers have maroon centers, and the disc flowers are interspersed with stiff hairs. The flowers close at night to protect their pollen.

Janet Horton

Common madia's strong turpentine scent is noticeable from a distance. The genus *Madia* includes oily plants that are also known as tarweeds; some species have been grown commercially for their oil. Common madia oil is marketed today as an aromatherapy essence. Indigenous Californians traditionally roast and grind the oil-rich seeds, which are then sometimes served as gruel.

SCIENTIFIC NAME	*Madia elegans* ssp. *elegans*
FAMILY	**Asteraceae** Sunflower
BLOOM	July–September

38 · Munz's Tidytips

Munz's tidytips are annuals adapted to the alkaline, clayey soils typical of vernal pools. They are daisylike, with thirteen yellow, three-lobed ray florets that have white outer tips.

Janet Horton

Larry Ulrich

The yellow disc flowers produce winged seeds called *achenes* that are different in shape from those of the ray flowers.

Once common in the inner Coast Ranges and San Joaquin Valley, they are seen less often as their habitat is converted to agriculture and developed as housing.

Philip Alexander Munz (1892–1974) was a botanist who taught at Pomona College and wrote many scientific texts and popular field guides about the flora of California.

SCIENTIFIC NAME	*Layia munzii*
FAMILY	**Asteraceae** Sunflower
BLOOM	March–April

39 · Three-rayed Tarweed

Keir Morse

Three-rayed tarweed is a common annual in the interior valleys and foothills. It bears a profusion of tiny flower heads, each with three ray florets and three disc florets.

Its common name, tarweed, is due to the strong scent of its glandular, needle-like leaves. However, there are dozens of other pungent members of the sunflower family that also have the common name of tarweed. The scientific, or Linnaean, system of classification assigns a unique name to every kind of plant. Due to the continued study of plant genetics, these names are occasionally revised. *Hemizonia lobbii* is now referred to as *Deinandra lobbii* in some sources.

SCIENTIFIC NAME	*Deinandra (Hemizonia) lobbii*
FAMILY	**Asteraceae** Sunflower
BLOOM	May–November

40 · Shrubby Butterweed, Ragwort, Groundsel

Keir Morse

Shrubby butterweed is a common perennial chaparral shrub that grows up to six feet tall. In late summer, the ends of its branches bear clusters of half-inch-wide flower heads, each with ten to thirteen rays. These flower heads produce seeds in fluffy white balls.

The plant has several common names, including threadleaf ragwort. *Senecio* comes from Latin *senex,* "old man," and refers to gray hairs on the plant's seeds.

Butterweeds are nectar plants for Mormon metalmark and mournful dusky wing butterflies. The nectar contains toxic alkaloids called pyrrolizidines that protect the butterflies from predators. Unfortunately, cattle that graze on *Senecio* species are also affected and suffer liver damage when they consume the plant.

SCIENTIFIC NAME	*Senecio flaccidus* var. *douglasii*
FAMILY	**Asteraceae** Sunflower
BLOOM	June–October

41 · Gray Mule-ears

Keir Morse

SCIENTIFIC NAME	*Wyethia helenioides*
FAMILY	**Asteraceae** Sunflower
BLOOM	March–July

Gray mule-ears are named for their floppy, fuzzy leaves that can be one to two feet long. They have one or a few large sunflower-like blossoms with twelve to eighteen yellow rays and large brown centers made up of disc flowers that are *perfect* (have both male and female parts in the same flower). They produce nutritious seeds, which are eaten by rodents and birds. Gray mule-ears emerge from a perennial taproot and are common on grassy plains and scrubby foothills.

Mule-ear flowers, like some other sunflowers, face the sun. An *auxin* (plant hormone) that regulates cell elongation accumulates on the shady side of the plant, causing the stem to bend toward the light.

42 · Whispering Bells

Whispering bells have dangling clusters of pale yellow, half-inch flowers with five petals fused into the shape of a bell. This bell-shaped corolla eventually dries out after blooming but remains on the plant. When breezes blow, the dried corollas make the soft, rustling sound that gives the plant its common name. Whispering bells have slender stalks and fernlike leaves with a medicinal fragrance.

Keir Morse

Whispering bells are another fire-following chaparral plant with seeds that are triggered to germinate by smoke. Unlike bush poppies and golden eardrops, however, they do not require an extended period in the soil first. Experiments show that it is the nitrogen dioxide in smoke that induces the germination of *Emmenanthe penduliflora*.

SCIENTIFIC NAME	*Emmenanthe penduliflora* var. *penduliflora*
FAMILY	**Hydrophyllaceae** Waterleaf
BLOOM	April–July

43 · Desert Dandelion, California Dandelion

Dave Welling

Many of us are accustomed to thinking of dandelions as noxious, invasive weeds, but there are a number of lovely native dandelions in California. The desert, or California, dandelion has fragrant, pale yellow flowers composed of overlapping ray florets spreading over a half-inch *involucre* (circle of bracts), the frilly "turtleneck" that all dandelions have. It does not have a center cluster of disc flowers.

Desert dandelions are annual flowers that respond to adequate rainfall with masses of yellow blooms in sandy grassland, chaparral, and oak woodland. *Malocothrix* has leaves at its base that are very woolly when young (*Malocothrix* comes from Greek *malakos*, "soft," and *thrix*, "hair").

SCIENTIFIC NAME	*Malocothrix californica*
FAMILY	**Asteraceae** Sunflower
BLOOM	March–May

44 · Yellow Pincushion

Yellow pincushions are in a sense the opposite of dandelions: They have many disc flowers but no true ray flowers. Their outer disc flowers, or florets, are enlarged, five-pointed cups with deep centers that do look a bit like rays, however. It is from these florets that the genus receives its name: *chaino* means "to gape" in Greek, and *aktis* means "ray."

Yellow pincushions are annuals that bloom in grassy valleys, foothills, and chaparral, including in dunes and serpentine soils. Some consider them to be fire followers. Although they do not depend upon fire or smoke for germination, they flourish when the ground is cleared of competing vegetation.

Keir Morse

SCIENTIFIC NAME	*Chaenactis glabriuscula* var. *glabriuscula*
FAMILY	**Asteraceae** Sunflower
BLOOM	March–May

45 · Rancher's Fireweed, Menzies' Fiddleneck

The small yellow or orange flowers of fiddleneck are made up of five petals fused into a cup and enclosed up to their chins by a bright green calyx. These are arranged along the side of a coiled stem and mature as the stem unfurls, an arrangement that gives this genus of plants its common name of fiddleneck. They produce seeds with small hooks that grab the fur of passing animals to achieve dispersal.

Menzies' fiddleneck is an abundant annual that germinates in the fall and blooms in open fields and grassy places—especially disturbed areas—in spring. Its sepals, stem, and leaves are covered with stiff white hairs that have a blister of granulated fluid at their bases. *Amsinckia* species contain thiaminase and pyrrolizidine alkaloids that can be toxic to grazing animals and irritating to human skin.

Charles Rettner

SCIENTIFIC NAME	*Amsinckia menziesii* var. *menziesii*
FAMILY	**Boraginaceae** Borage
BLOOM	April–June

46 · Honeysuckle

Honeysuckle is a perennial chaparral vine with pairs of simple leaves neatly spaced along its stems. Its pale yellow flowers bloom in terminal clusters of two to six. These flowers have long, back-curled lips—the upper with four lobes and the lower with one—with five yellow stamens protruding from the tube of the corolla. They have a sweet, honeylike fragrance.

Honeysuckle belongs to the same family as another common chaparral plant, blue elderberry (*Sambucus mexicana*). They both produce berries, but people commonly eat or ferment as beverages only the ones from the elderberry. Honeysuckle is the host plant of the bumblebee clearwing moth, a day-flying sphinx moth that mimics bumblebees.

Keir Morse

SCIENTIFIC NAME	*Lonicera subspicata* var. *denudata*
FAMILY	**Caprifoliaceae** Honeysuckle
BLOOM	April–June

47 · Bladder Parsnip, Common Lomatium

Keir Morse

The five-petaled flowers of bladder parsnip are tiny, but they are massed in showy clusters called *umbels,* which in this case are further clustered into larger umbels. Compound umbels such as these provide a good landing platform for the bees that frequent this family of plants.

Bladder parsnip is a perennial of the chaparral, open grassy slopes, meadows, and woodland. It has a thick taproot like its relatives: carrots, parsnips, and celery. Its ferny leaves resemble another relative, parsley, and its strong fragrance has lent it another common name of hog fennel. Bladder parsnip is the host plant for anise swallowtail butterflies. Rodents eat its roots, rabbits eat its leaves, and many creatures eat its large and oily seeds.

SCIENTIFIC NAME	*Lomatium utriculatum*
FAMILY	**Apiaceae** Carrot
BLOOM	February–May

48 · Sanicle, Snakeroot

SCIENTIFIC NAME	*Sanicula crassicaulis*
FAMILY	**Apiaceae** Carrot
BLOOM	March–May

Mark Turner

Sanicle's compound umbrels of yellowish-brown flowers bloom in mild habitats such as oak woodlands, ravines, and moist-phase chaparral. Its stout, single stem emerges from a perennial taproot and can be more than four feet tall, flourishing in rich soil or in clay. The leaves are *palmate* (divided like the fingers of a hand).

Sanicle fruits have little hooked prickles on them, which facilitate their dispersal by birds over great distances. With the help of DNA analysis, researchers have discovered descendants of *Sanicula crassicaulis* in South America, which they believe evolved from seeds transported there from California by migrating birds.

49 · Valley Tassels

Valley tassels are grassland annuals that germinate in the fall and blossom in the spring. In any given year, there may be thousands of them or only a few. The flowers are nestled among numerous white bracts near the tops of two- to twelve-inch spikes. Each blossom has yellow, balloonlike pouches between an upper "beak" and a small lower lip. Purplish dots on these pouches make them look like faces.

Valley tassels are hemi-parasitic rather than true parasitic plants. This means that although their roots take nutrients from the roots of other plants, they do not derive all of their nourishment by this means. The plants also photosynthesize carbohydrates from water and carbon dioxide on their own.

Charles Rettner

SCIENTIFIC NAME	*Castilleja attenuata*
FAMILY	**Scrophulariaceae** Figwort
BLOOM	March–May

50 · Hoary Nettle

Hoary nettle, a perennial riparian plant, can reach eight feet in height. It has triangular leaves that are from one to three inches long, and the entire plant is covered with small hairs. These hairs have slanted tips that break off easily and become embedded in skin. They carry a toxic fluid that causes an immediate rash. (*Urtica* comes from Latin *uro*, "I burn.")

The species name, *dioica*, means that the female and male flowers bloom on separate plants. Both are inconspicuous and hang in branching clusters. Female flowers have no petals and hang in spikes that are 1/2 to 2 inches long, while male flowers have four sepals and four petals, and their spikes may be twice as long.

Hoary nettle is a host plant for satyr comma, red admiral, painted lady, and west coast lady butterflies.

Keir Morse

SCIENTIFIC NAME	*Urtica dioica* ssp. *holosericea*
FAMILY	**Urticaceae** Nettle
BLOOM	June–September

51 · Deerweed

Keir Morse

Deerweed is a chaparral plant that helps to heal fire-ravaged slopes. It holds exposed soil in place, and the nitrogen-fixing microorganisms on its roots enrich it. A perennial, it is common after fires but is eventually replaced by other plants.

Lotus scoparius bears clusters of yellow pea flowers in whorls around its stems. These flowers, which attract a variety of bees, become reddish with age and produce a curved seedpod with a hook on the end. The caterpillars of burnet moths ingest cyanogenic glycosides from members of the genus *Lotus* (Greek for a mythical fruit that induced amnesia). These glycosides persist in the adult moth and protect it from birds. Deerweed is host for western green hairstreak, eastern tailed blue, marine blue, Acmon blue, and silvery blue butterflies.

SCIENTIFIC NAME	*Lotus scoparius* var. *scoparius*
FAMILY	**Fabaceae** Legume
BLOOM	March–August

52 · California False Lupine, Golden Pea

Christopher Christie

After the periodic fires that sweep through the chaparral, the hollow stems of California false lupine readily resprout from an underground bud. A single plant may produce hundreds of seeds, but these have very hard coats and do not germinate readily. They must be heated to 175°F or else *scarified* (deeply scratched, usually by tumbling over gravel during a rainstorm).

False lupine is a favorite of huge bees like carpenter bees and bumblebees. Each shrub has several spikes encircled with as many as one hundred pea-shaped flowers, each about 2/3 inch long. It is distinguished from true lupines by its leaves, which have only three leaflets whereas lupines have several.

SCIENTIFIC NAME	*Thermopsis macrophylla*
FAMILY	**Fabaceae** Legume
BLOOM	April–June

53 · Common Monkeyflower

SCIENTIFIC NAME	*Mimulus guttatus*
FAMILY	**Scrophulariaceae** Figwort
BLOOM	March–August

Common monkeyflower thrives in wet places. The plants are quite variable: They may be small, bushy, tall, scrawny, leafy, or any combination of these. The flowers range from 1/2 to 1 1/2 inches in length. Depending upon conditions, they may be either annual or perennial.

Dave Welling

Common monkeyflowers have bright yellow snapdragon "faces" with red spots sprinkled in their throats that apparently serve as a guide for pollinating bees. The flowers can last six days, but they shrivel sooner when pollen is deposited on their stigmas. If no pollinator visits, the flower pollinates itself after a few days. Self-pollination means the survival of that plant's genetic material, but it is less beneficial for the species as a whole. Without the mixing of DNA, *Mimulus* and other flowers are less capable of evolving to accommodate change.

54 · Johnny Jump-up

Charles Rettner

Johnny jump-ups are little yellow violets that bloom on open, grassy slopes in blue oak woodlands and chaparral. They have five petals with dark marks in their centers, purple on the front and brown on the back. All twenty-three species of *Viola* in California are edible, but the insects that consume their nectar and pollen—as well as the birds, rodents, and rabbits that eat their seeds—need them more than people do.

Johnny jump-ups are a host for several species of fritillary butterflies, which lay their eggs on the dried leaves. When the caterpillars emerge the following spring, they feed on the plant, resting, growing, and shedding their skins. Then they stitch leaves together into a chamber in which they pupate for two weeks, emerging as adult butterflies that live for about three weeks between mid-May and late July.

SCIENTIFIC NAME	*Viola pedunculata*
FAMILY	**Violaceae** Violet
BLOOM	February–April

55 · California Poppy

Dave Welling

California poppies are emblems of the California grasslands. When they bloom, they push off a cone-shaped sepal that drops to the ground, releasing four fan-shaped, yellow to bright orange petals that unfurl to release a spicy fragrance. Beetles are attracted by this fragrance to eat the poppy's pollen, getting enough of it dusted on them to pollinate the next poppy that they visit. When enough of the flowers are massed in one area, they are showy enough to draw bumblebees also.

As evening approaches or when the weather is wet or cloudy, California poppies furl their petals together to protect their pollen from being washed away or consumed by the "wrong" pollinator. They produce long, slender seed capsules that pop open in dry weather and scatter little black seeds. The plant is toxic to humans.

SCIENTIFIC NAME	*Eschscholzia californica*
FAMILY	**Papaveraceae** Poppy
BLOOM	February–September

56 · Wind Poppy

Wind poppies resemble California poppies, which are in the same family. Both have four orange petals, but their stigmas are very obviously different. The stigmas of the wind poppy are gathered into a protruding head on a slender style in order to make contact with the light, pollen-dusted bodies of bees. The stigmas of the California poppy are flat on the pod instead, to come in contact with the heavy bodies of beetles. The intense orange of wind poppies is produced by plant pigments called *carotenoids*, which protect plant cells from excessive solar radiation.

Heterophylla means having different leaves on the same plant. Wind poppies have leaves that are *pinnate* (like a feather, with branches opposite a center line). Some of these leaves are further divided into fernlike foliage.

SCIENTIFIC NAME	*Stylomecon heterophylla*
FAMILY	**Papaveraceae** Poppy
BLOOM	April–May

Larry Ulrich

57 · Western Wallflower

Wallflowers receive their common name from their tendency to grow next to walls or rocks or on steep slopes. Like others in its genus, the western wallflower is a *biennial* or a short-lived perennial. A biennial is merely a rosette of leaves during its first year and produces blossoms in its second year.

Janet Horton

Terminal clusters of fragrant flowers bloom progressively up its stalk, attracting various long-tongued pollinators such as bees, wasps, long-tongued flies, moths, and butterflies. Western tiger swallowtail butterflies especially favor them. *Erysimum* species also host several species of white butterflies. Nectar is produced only when the flower first opens.

Members of Brassicaceae produce pollen with a protein on it that will not allow the flowers to self-fertilize.

SCIENTIFIC NAME	*Erysimum capitatum* var. *capitatum*
FAMILY	**Brassicaceae** Mustard
BLOOM	March–July

58 · Sticky Monkeyflower

Sticky monkeyflower is a common woody perennial subshrub in rocky chaparral, open woods, canyon slopes, and disturbed areas. Its branches are covered with a tacky varnish that protects the plant from moisture loss and enables it to flourish in dry conditions that are the opposite of those favored by its close relative, the common monkeyflower of seeps and streams.

Janet Horton

Sticky monkeyflower is a good source of nectar for hummingbirds, its primary pollinators. The stigma of each flower has two lobes that close in response to touch. If the contact deposits pollen, the flower takes thirty to ninety minutes to close and usually remains shut, presumably to protect the newly deposited pollen. If there is no pollen, the flowers reopen within four hours or so. Sticky monkeyflowers are host to the variable checkerspot butterfly.

SCIENTIFIC NAME	*Mimulus aurantiacus*
FAMILY	**Scrophulariaceae** Figwort
BLOOM	March–June

59 · Red Maids

Red maids are sprawling, semi-succulent annuals that require moist soil. Their ephemeral flowers need bright sunlight to bloom and close when shade passes over them. These flowers are *perfect*, meaning that both stamens and pistils are in the same flower. They are also like a child's image of a "perfect" flower—with five simple red petals in a shallow bowl shape that is just half an inch across. *Ciliata*, "eyelash," describes the slight fringing of their petals.

Red maids produce hard little black seeds sometimes ground into flour by indigenous Californians. The leaves are edible too, either raw or cooked.

SCIENTIFIC NAME	*Calandrinia ciliata*
FAMILY	**Portulacaceae** Purslane
BLOOM	February–May

60 · California Catchfly, Indian Pink

Indian pinks are not pink; the common name refers to the serrated, or "pinked," edges of their bright red petals. They are perennial, isolated bloomers in rocky, open oak woodland and coniferous forest. The flowers are one to two inches wide with five petals, a fused tubular calyx with five teeth, and edible seeds.

The upper stems are coated with a gummy secretion that is probably the source of the generic name from the Greek Silenus, a slobbering companion of Bacchus. This secretion traps very small insects, such as gnats and ants, preventing them from reaching the flower and leading to another common name for the plant, catchfly.

SCIENTIFIC NAME	*Silene californica*
FAMILY	**Caryophyllaceae** Carnation
BLOOM	May–July

61 · Lance-leaved Dudleya

Janet Horton

Lance-leaved dudleya is a perennial plant that stores moisture in its fleshy leaves. (Its family name comes from Latin *crassus*, meaning "thick"). This enables it to thrive in the harsh habitat of rock and scree. Its yellow-red flowers have five petals that form a tube, a shape favored by their hummingbird pollinators. Dudleyas are host plants for the Sonoran blue butterfly, whose caterpillar burrows into their thick leaves and feeds on their succulent flesh.

The family Crassulaceae often reproduces vegetatively by sending up new plants from its roots to grow beside the "mother" plant. This avoids the difficulty of establishing seedlings in harsh environments, but it does not enable the beneficial mixing of genetic material between plants.

Dudleyas are named for William Dudley (1849–1911), the first botany professor and head of the Botany Department at Stanford University.

SCIENTIFIC NAME	*Dudleya lanceolata*
FAMILY	**Crassulaceae** Stonecrop
BLOOM	April–July

62 · Venus Thistle, Cobwebby Thistle

Venus thistles are endemic to California. Their two-inch-wide flowers look like soft round brushes at the tips of their stems, which may be as tall as six feet. The long white hairs tangled in these flowers give them another common name, cobwebby thistle. Venus thistles attract hummingbirds and swallowtail butterflies and are hosts to the painted lady butterfly. Although Venus thistle is a chaparral perennial with a thick taproot, the plant usually dies after an especially vigorous bloom. Its stems are tough and fibrous and are used by indigenous Californians for baskets and cordage.

Keir Morse

SCIENTIFIC NAME	*Cirsium occidentale* var. *venustum*
FAMILY	**Asteraceae** Sunflower
BLOOM	May–July

63 · Scarlet Bugler

Keir Morse

Scarlet bugler is dainty and ethereal, strong and bright. It is a perennial with red, tubular flowers that bloom in summer to appeal to hummingbirds. The flowers are an inch or two long, made up of five petals that are fused almost completely except for short lobes at the open ends. They blossom near the tops of thin stems, which can be up to four feet tall and have pairs of long, narrow leaves along their length.

Like others in their genus, scarlet buglers are commonly found in disturbed soils that have been scraped, flooded, or denuded of other vegetation that might compete with them for moisture and nutrients. Road cuts and construction sites are often colonized by penstemons.

SCIENTIFIC NAME	*Penstemon centranthifolius*
FAMILY	**Scrophulariaceae** Figwort
BLOOM	April–June

64 · California Figwort, California Bee Plant

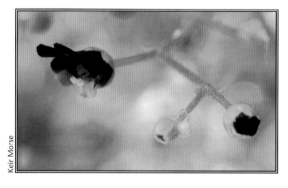

Keir Morse

California figwort appeals to bees so much that its other common name is California bee plant. The somber maroon blossoms have markings that reflect ultraviolet light to produce a color that bees can see but we humans cannot.

This perennial's relatively lush appearance indicates its moist habitat. It is tolerant of serpentine soils. It has serrated, triangular leaves that diminish in size higher on the stem, which may be three to six feet tall. These host the caterpillars of variable checkerspot butterflies, which sequester the plant's iridoid toxins as a defense against predators.

SCIENTIFIC NAME	*Scrophularia californica* var. *floribunda*
FAMILY	**Scrophulariaceae** Figwort
BLOOM	February–July

SCIENTIFIC NAME	*Pedicularis densiflora*
FAMILY	**Scrophulariaceae** Figwort
BLOOM	January–June

Larry Ulrich

Indian warrior is an early bloomer in chaparral and forested areas. When its frilly, fernlike leaves first emerge they are copper colored, indicating that the plant is not producing enough chlorophyll to make adequate food through *photosynthesis* (using sunlight to convert water and carbon dioxide into carbohydrates). Instead, Indian warrior partially parasitizes the roots of another plant, usually chamise.

Being a perennial gives the plant a jump start on the season; being partially parasitic gives it an early source of nourishment and moisture to sustain it while flowering and helps to make Indian warrior tolerant of nutrient-poor serpentine soils.

Indian warrior is host to the Edith's checkerspot butterfly. Checkerspot butterflies also feed on the nectar of its dark red flowers.

66 · Indian Paintbrush

Indian paintbrush is common in dry woodlands, chaparral slopes, and coastal scrub. The showy red parts of its flower heads are really modified leaves called *bracts*, which surround the true flower in a supporting role.

The flowers themselves protrude from a red, toothed calyx but appear yellow, with a slender, inch-long, slightly shaggy tube called a *beak* above a lower lip that is green or violet. Indian paintbrush is pollinated by hummingbirds, who are rewarded with nectar produced by the flowers but are actually attracted to the plant by the showy but unproductive red bracts.

Indian paintbrush is the host plant for variable and Edith's checkerspot butterflies.

Larry Ulrich

SCIENTIFIC NAME	*Castilleja affinis* ssp. *affinis*
FAMILY	**Scrophulariaceae** Figwort
BLOOM	March–May

67 · California Fuchsia, Zauschneria, Hummingbird Trumpet

Keir Morse

California fuchsia presents its hummingbird visitors with a long, funnel-shaped red calyx that contains nectar at its bulging base. The flower's petals are the same color, spreading from the throat of this calyx like a scarlet petticoat. Most important to the flower, its pollen-receiving stigmas and pollen-bearing anthers are *exserted* (protruding) well beyond the petals. These vital flower parts are in position to receive pollen or to deposit it on the feathers of a hummingbird whenever one hovers close to sip its nectar.

A perennial subshrub, California fuchsia is found in the chaparral or other dry slope and ridge habitats. Its seeds are beaked, with a tuft of hairs to aid in wind dispersal or to catch in passing fur.

SCIENTIFIC NAME	*Epilobium canum* ssp. *canum*
FAMILY	**Onagraceae** Evening Primrose
BLOOM	August–October

68 · Western Columbine

Janet Horton

Western columbine beckons hummingbirds to open woods, stream banks, and seeps. Its flowers have five spreading red sepals to attract attention and five yellow petals that have tubes called *spurs* extending back from the face of the flower to a knobby bulge containing nectar. The flower's openings face down, so that hummingbirds are dusted with pollen from numerous yellow stamens as they probe for nectar.

Columbines produce lots of tiny black seeds in long pods. These pods crack open when they dry to broadcast the seeds not far from the mother plant. Seeds that are not consumed by animals are stimulated by sunlight to germinate on the surface of the soil.

The common name columbine is from the Latin *columbinus,* "dove," for the resemblance of the petals to a circle of doves.

SCIENTIFIC NAME	*Aquilegia formosa*
FAMILY	**Ranunculaceae** Buttercup
BLOOM	May–August

Four-spots are annuals with simple, deep pink flowers that bloom in open, grassy, or shrubby areas. Often, each of the flowers' four petals has a darker spot at the tip or above the middle of each petal, giving the flowers both their common name and their specific epithet *quadrivulnera,* which means "four wounds" in Latin. Four-spots are popular with bees.

The genus *Clarkia* first arose in California and most of the thirty *Clarkia* species are still endemic to the state. It was named for William Clark (1770–1838) who with Meriwether Lewis led the famous exploration of North America from 1804 to 1806. Four-spot is in a group of Clarkias known as *Godetia,* which have petals that are broad rather than narrow at the base.

Deidra Walpole

SCIENTIFIC NAME	*Clarkia purpurea* ssp. *quadrivulnera*
FAMILY	**Onagraceae** Evening Primrose
BLOOM	April–July

Elegant clarkia is a striking flower with four glowing magenta petals that are *clawed*—very narrow at their base—and spread into fan shapes at their outer ends. *(Unguiculata* is Latin for "little red claw.") It has four conspicuous, bright red anthers as well as four white ones on shorter filaments, and its white stigma pokes out in front of the flower on a long style. The four reddish sepals turn to one side after the flower opens, forming a shell-like cup under it. This elaborate blossom is pollinated by bees.

Charles Rettner

Elegant clarkia is a perennial chaparral plant that blooms in summer and is common along roadsides. Indigenous Californians have long collected *Clarkia* seeds, parched them, and ground them into meal.

SCIENTIFIC NAME	*Clarkia unguiculata*
FAMILY	**Onagraceae** Evening Primrose
BLOOM	May–July

71 · California Rose

Dave Welling

Rosa californica is the archetypal rose. It is deep pink, simple, with five roundish petals and numerous fine stamens bearing anthers with dusty yellow pollen. California wild rose is a perennial that favors riparian areas, either climbing over other plants or forming a shrub that is three to six feet high.

Roses technically do not have *thorns,* which are sharpened stems, or *spines,* which are modified leaves. Their stems are covered in *prickles* (sharp growths produced from their skin).

SCIENTIFIC NAME	*Rosa californica*
FAMILY	**Rosaceae** Rose
BLOOM	May–August

The rose family is an important source of edible fruits, including apples, strawberries, blackberries, pears, plums, peaches, and apricots. California wild rose develops edible fruits called rose hips, which are rich in Vitamin C. It is one of several host plants for the gray hairstreak butterfly.

72 · Bitter Root

Discovering bitter root blossoming in the harsh habitat of rock and scree can seem as improbable as finding ballerinas on the moon. Yet bitter root grows in a wide range of often challenging conditions from rocky ground to talus slopes, sage-brush scrub to open woodlands. It thrives in serpentine, clay, and granite soils.

The delicate flowers—each with twelve to eighteen tissuelike, evanescent pink petals and six to eight peach-colored sepals—bloom on a thick, leafless stem that emerges from a perennial taproot. They blossom in early summer as the rosette of narrow, succulent leaves that encircles the plant dies. Bitter root opens only in sunshine and withers quickly.

The specific name, *Lewisia rediviva,* means "brought back to life" in Latin. The genus was named for Captain Meriwether Lewis (1774–1809) of the Lewis and Clark Expedition.

Dave Welling

SCIENTIFIC NAME	*Lewisia rediviva*
FAMILY	**Portulacaceae** Purslane
BLOOM	March–June

73 · Slender-flowered Gilia

Keir Morse

SCIENTIFIC NAME	*Gilia tenuiflora* ssp. *tenuiflora*
FAMILY	**Polemoniaceae** Phlox
BLOOM	April–June

Slender-flowered gilia is an annual that grows in sandy washes, canyons, and riparian areas in otherwise desertlike country. It has a pinkish or violet-blue flower with five petals that form a tube at their base. Bees are attracted to its pale center, which they probe for pollen. Many Polemoniaceae have blue pollen and bees that collect it often specialize in flowers with blue pollen.

Slender-flowered gilia produces many seeds. These have coats that develop a mucilaginous slime when wet. This mucilage retains the moisture long enough to soften the seed coat and result in germination. Soil adheres to this sticky surface and conceals the seeds from rodents that would eat them.

The genus *Gilia* is named for Filippo Luigi Gilii (1756–1821), an Italian naturalist, clergyman, and director of the Vatican Observatory.

74 · Pink Spineflower

Pink spineflowers bloom in grasslands, foothill woodlands, and chaparral, especially in sandy and well-drained areas. They form rounded clusters on delicate stems that repeatedly fork into nearly equal branches.

Like other members of the buckwheat family, spineflowers do not have petals. What look like urn-shaped corollas are actually six hairy bracts fused together to protect a woolly little calyx that has six segments enclosing an ovary and nine stamens. Pink spineflowers are fragrant annuals that attract flies, wasps, at least six species of butterflies, and bees—including leaf-cutter bees.

Keir Morse

SCIENTIFIC NAME	*Chorizanthe membranacea*
FAMILY	**Polygonaceae** Buckwheat
BLOOM	April–July

75 · Pitcher Sage

Janet Horton

Pitcher sage is a common, perennial subshrub of the woodlands and chaparral that can reach five feet in height. Like many other members of the mint family, pitcher sage has stems that are square in cross-section as well as strongly scented, fuzzy leaves, which in this case have prominent veins and wavy edges. It has a range of pollinators, including Chalcedon checkerspot butterflies.

The name pitcher sage comes from the spouted jug shape of its pink or white flowers, formed of five fused petals with the lowest a bit longer than the others. *Calycina* refers to the calyx, which encloses the base of the flower in a green cup with five triangular lobes. Its terminal clusters of one-inch flowers last for only a few days. After the flower wilts, the calyx inflates and becomes papery and persistent.

SCIENTIFIC NAME	*Lepechinia calycina*
FAMILY	**Lamiaceae** Mint
BLOOM	April–June

76 · Chaparral Pea

Chaparral pea is well adapted to its dry, fire-prone chaparral habitat. Its leaves are small, hard, and leathery to reduce moisture loss. It resprouts after burns from a root crown that grows larger after each fire. As with other members of its family, the roots have nodules supporting nitrogen-fixing bacteria that enrich the soil.

Pickeringia montana forms hillside thickets of spiny branches that can reach eight feet in height. These intimidating shrubs burst into bloom with bright reddish-purple pea flowers about 3/4 inch long.

Pickeringia is named in honor of a Philadelphia physician and botanist named Charles Pickering (1805–1878), who came to California with the Wilkes expedition in 1841. *Montana* is the only species in this genus, and this variety is limited to California.

Janet Horton

SCIENTIFIC NAME	*Pickeringia montana* var. *montana*
FAMILY	**Fabaceae** Legume
BLOOM	May–August

77 · Pinpoint Clover

Keir Morse

Pinpoint clover is a delicate-looking annual that blooms in open, often disturbed places and serpentine soils in grassland, chaparral, oak woodland, and occasionally desert. It bears terminal clusters of pinkish-lavender pea flowers that resemble crowns with pale tips. Pea flowers have a broad upper petal called a *banner,* two side petals called *wings,* and two bottom petals that are joined in the shape of a boat's hull and are known as a *keel.*

Trifolium is the genus that most of us call clovers. Its members have compound leaves, generally with three leaflets—*Trifolium* is Latin for "three leaves." Clover flowers have a sweet scent and are high in nectar. They attract a variety of insects and bees, including honeybees, which make especially good honey from clover nectar.

SCIENTIFIC NAME	*Trifolium gracilentum* var. *gracilentum*
FAMILY	**Fabaceae** Legume
BLOOM	April–June

78 · Purple Owl's-clover

SCIENTIFIC NAME	*Castilleja exserta* ssp. *exserta*
FAMILY	**Scrophulariaceae** Figwort
BLOOM	March–May

Owl's-clover is not really a clover and is not even in the same family; its flower heads merely resemble some members of *Trifolium.* Instead, it is closely related to Indian paintbrush and valley tassles. Like those other members of the genus *Castilleja,* it is hemi-parasitic on the roots of other plants and its flowers also bloom amid modified leaves called *bracts.*

The deep pink bracts of owl's-clover have white or yellow tips. They surround pink flowers that have an upper beak and a broad lower lip with a white tip and yellow dots that look a bit like the eyes of an owl.

Owl's-clover is an annual that is often mixed in open grasslands with poppies, lupines, and goldfields.

Larry Ulrich

79 · Baby Blue-eyes

Larry Ulrich

SCIENTIFIC NAME	*Nemophila menziesii* var. *menziesii*
FAMILY	**Hydrophyllaceae** Waterleaf
BLOOM	February–June

Baby blue-eyes are annuals that bloom in grasslands, chaparral, woodlands, and desert washes. Their flowers have five lobed petals in a bowl shape with a pale center. Their coloration varies a great deal from place to place.

Flowers generally attract pollinators with color and scent. But as the flower physiologist Friedrich Barth points out, "Once one has arrived at the restaurant, one must find the door." Most flowers have markings—combinations of lines, dots, and shadings—that direct insects to the source of the nectar they are seeking. Colored veins and black dots lead insects into the pale centers of baby blue-eyes.

80 · Blue Fiesta Flower

Janet Horton

SCIENTIFIC NAME	*Pholistoma auritum* var. *auritum*
FAMILY	**Hydrophyllaceae** Waterleaf
BLOOM	March–May

Blue fiesta flower is a weak-stemmed annual with fragile, curved prickles that enable it to straggle, matlike, over other plants or boulders in its moist and shady habitat. Its five petals are actually deep lavender or purple rather than blue, and are pale toward the center of the blossom. Blue fiesta flower is a close cousin to baby blue-eyes and was once placed in the same genus. *Pholistoma membranaceum* is a close relative that blooms on the Carrizo Plain.

The leaves of fiesta flower are unusual. They are divided into long lobes, the bottom ones fused to the stem like ears (*auritum* means "eared" in Latin).

81 · Shooting Star

Shooting star is one of the very earliest flowers to appear, emerging from moist soil in meadows and oak woodlands. Its family name comes from the Latin *primula veris*, "little firstling of spring." It is a true primrose with five sepals and five petals, which are bent back sharply from their united base as though the blossom has been turned inside out. The flowers bloom in clusters at the ends of their stems and may be a pinkish violet or white. Their European cousins, the cyclamens, are grown as ornamentals.

Dodecatheon comes from the Greek *dodeka*, "twelve," and *thios*, "gods." The reasons for this name are unclear, but it was used by the ancient Roman naturalist Pliny for a European member of the primrose family.

Larry Ulrich

SCIENTIFIC NAME	*Dodecatheon clevelandii* ssp. *patulum*
FAMILY	**Primulaceae** Primrose
BLOOM	January–March

82 · Blue Witch, Chaparral Nightshade

The flowers of blue witch are five-pointed stars with bright yellow anthers clustered together in the center, the petals united into a tube at the back. They blossom in clusters on branch tips of a perennial subshrub that has gray, hairy foliage to reduce moisture loss in its dry woodland and chaparral environments. Although they are mostly early summer bloomers, some may be found blossoming most of the year.

Blue witch belongs to an interesting family that provides many important foods but also some significant poisons. Tomatoes and eggplant belong to this family, but so do tobacco, jimson weed, and deadly nightshade. Blue witch shares with its fellow members of *Solanum* a complex of toxins including solanine and solasonine, which have potentially fatal effects several hours after ingestion.

Keir Morse

SCIENTIFIC NAME	*Solanum umbelliferum*
FAMILY	**Solanaceae** Nightshade
BLOOM	May–June

83 · Blue-eyed Grass

Janet Horton

Like other members of the iris family, blue-eyed grass has narrow leaves with parallel (instead of branching) veins. Its three sepals and three petals are fused together in a *perianth*—a floral structure combining a calyx and corolla—in which there is there is no marked differentiation between them.

Blue-eyed grass is a common flower in open, grassy areas and woodlands. Summer dormant, it appears to die back completely during the dry months. It is a perennial, however, with a fibrous rootstock that rests until winter rains replenish its moisture and lengthening hours of sunlight prompt it to bloom again in spring. The plant needs its rest. When gardeners plant it in their gardens and water it all summer, it usually does not survive to bloom again.

SCIENTIFIC NAME	*Sisyrinchium bellum*
FAMILY	Iridaceae Iris
BLOOM	March–May

84 · Douglas Iris

Douglas irises form clumps of sword-like leaves on grassy slopes and in the open brush. These tough, fibrous leaves are folded and overlapping and may be up to three feet long. They continue to be an important source of fiber for baskets and cordage made by indigenous Californians. The plant has a very bitter taste and, when brewed into a tea, has been used to induce vomiting.

Dave Welling

Douglas iris emerges from perennial rootstocks or *rhizomes,* which are not true roots but actually underground stems. It is an adaptable plant found throughout the Coast Ranges from Oregon to Santa Barbara and is tolerant of serpentine soils. The flowers have three sepals that curve downward and three narrower, upright petals of about the same length.

SCIENTIFIC NAME	*Iris douglasiana*
FAMILY	Iridaceae Iris
BLOOM	March–May

85 · Ithuriel's Spear

Ithuriel's spear is a perennial plant that varies widely in size and in the color of its flowers. These flowers have three sepals, three petals, three long stamens, and three shorter stamens. (*Triteleia* is Greek for "three complete.") They are attached by short stalks called *pedicels* to form clusters on the ends of long *scapes,* or leafless stems. These scapes, in turn, arise from an edible *corm,* a globular, underground stem. Ithuriel's spear may be found in grassland, open forest, and woodlands.

The common name comes from Milton's *Paradise Lost,* in which an angel named Ithuriel finds Satan disguised as a toad in the Garden of Eden, next to a sleeping Eve. When Ithuriel touches the toad with his spear, Satan resumes his true appearance.

Larry Ulrich

SCIENTIFIC NAME	*Triteleia laxa*
FAMILY	Liliaceae Lily
BLOOM	May–July

86 · Elegant Brodiaea

Most elegant brodiaea plants wait to blossom until their *corms* (underground stems) have stored nutrients for four or five years. Then in summer, just as the native grasses are drying out and its own few straplike leaves have withered, elegant brodiaea produces umbels of bluish-purple to violet flowers on pedicels at the tops of stout, foot-tall scapes.

Brodiaea corms are nutritious and have a nutty taste long enjoyed by indigenous Californians. These corms are covered with dark brown fibers and multiply to form "daughter" corms that bring forth more plants. Rodents also consume the corms as well as the large seeds produced by the flowers.

Elegant brodiaea is common on the dry, rolling plains and grassy slopes of the western Sierra Nevada foothills. The genus *Brodiaea* is named for James Brodie (1744–1824), a Scottish botanist.

Dave Welling

SCIENTIFIC NAME	*Brodiaea elegans*
FAMILY	Liliaceae Lily
BLOOM	May–June

87 · Blue Dicks

Janet Horton

SCIENTIFIC NAME	*Dichelostemma capitatum* ssp. *capitatum*
FAMILY	**Liliaceae** Lily
BLOOM	March–May

Blue dicks are another perennial lily with an edible bulb. Their flower parts occur in multiples of three. Blue dicks bloom in open oak woodlands, chaparral, grassland, and desert, forming globular clusters of three to fifteen cup-shaped, six-pointed flowers on a single flower stalk that may reach a foot in height. They are one of California's most common wildflowers in early spring, but their grasslike leaves have usually dried up by the time they bloom.

The bulbs of blue dicks have a nutty flavor and were an important source of carbohydrates in earlier times. Miwok and other peoples dig them up and bake them in earth ovens.

88 · Many-flowered Eriastrum

Many-flowered eriastrum are annuals that produce beautiful, blue-purple flowers on some of the driest flats and slopes in chaparral, woodlands, and pine forests. The plants are able to endure these conditions partly because of the woolliness that buffers them from the sun and drying winds (Greek *erion,* "wool," and *astrum,* "star"). They also have very thin foliage that looks delicate but is fibrous.

The flowers are shiny, with five petals that are fused at their bases into a short tube. These form spherical clusters (*pluriflorum* means "many-flowered") at the ends of nearly leafless stems. Like many other members of the phlox family, they produce blue pollen.

Christopher Christie

SCIENTIFIC NAME	*Eriastrum pluriflorum*
FAMILY	**Polemoniaceae** Phlox
BLOOM	May–July

89 · Lax Snapdragon

Lax snapdragons are annual chaparral plants with flowers that look like sleek, scaled-back garden snapdragons. They have five fused petals with a bulged lower lip that has fuzzy hairs on it. Bees and other insects seeking nectar from the snapdragon must be strong enough to push their way into the throat of the flower. The genus name comes from the Greek *anti,* "rivaling" or "simulating" and *rhinon,* "noselike," because of the snouted faces of its members.

Antirrhinum kelloggii blooms in years of adequate rainfall, which may not occur for decades. Its seeds bide their time in the soil until conditions are right. The plant responds to fire and colonizes burned areas with wiry, vinelike upper stems.

Keir Morse

SCIENTIFIC NAME	*Antirrhinum kelloggii*
FAMILY	**Scrophulariaceae** Figwort
BLOOM	March–May

90 · Parry's Larkspur

Parry's larkspur is very common in the moist grasslands, chaparral, and oak woodlands of the southern half of California. It has hairy, stiff, hollow stems and deeply divided leaves. The plant grows from a short trunk called a *caudex,* which arises from woody perennial roots.

When spikes of Parry's larkspur bloom, the showy parts of each flower are its five blue sepals. The upper one has a half-inch spur projecting toward the back, which gives the plant its common name. Four small, cuplike petals are paired in the flower's center; the upper ones have nectar-bearing spurs extending back into the calyx tube.

The blue flower pigment delphinidin is named for its occurrence in this genus. Delphiniums also contain very toxic alkaloids, including delphinine, which are poisonous to livestock and humans.

Keir Morse

SCIENTIFIC NAME	*Delphinium parryi* ssp. *parryi*
FAMILY	**Ranunculaceae** Buttercup
BLOOM	April–May

91 · Fleabane Daisy

Larry Ulrich

These simple, inch-wide flowers with their threadlike leaves may look like occasional annuals, but their foot-long stems grow from a branched crown on a short, perennial taproot. The plants spend winters as rosettes of long, thin leaves.

Fleabane daisies bloom in clusters in open, rocky grasslands, moist chaparral, coniferous forests, and along streams. At night, their fifteen to sixty ray flowers bend together to protect their yellow disc flowers; they reopen in the morning. These flowers produce many seeds with attached plumes, in a fluffy white head. *Erigeron* is from Greek *eri,* "early," and *geron,* "old man," and means "old man in the spring." The common name comes from the use of the plant to repel fleas.

SCIENTIFIC NAME	*Erigeron foliosus* var. *foliosus*
FAMILY	**Asteraceae** Sunflower
BLOOM	April–August

92 · Houndstongue

Charles Rettner

SCIENTIFIC NAME	*Cynoglossum grande*
FAMILY	**Boraginaceae** Borage
BLOOM	February–April

Both the Latin and common names of this spring forget-me-not come from its four- to six-inch-long oval leaves rather than its flowers. (*Cynoglossum* is from the Greek *kynos,* "dog," and *glossa,* "tongue.") The flowers have blue petals with white, tooth-like appendages where they meet in the center. These form a crownlike target for bees seeking nectar. Houndstongue is fairly common in moist, shady places. The plant becomes dormant in autumn.

Many members of Boraginaceae are poisonous. Houndstongue contains the toxic alkaloid cynoglossine.

93 · Miniature Lupine

Miniature lupine often mixes with California poppies on rolling grasslands and oak woodlands, especially in damp areas. It is an abundant annual that germinates when the winter rains begin and blooms in spring. The blossoms are typical pea flowers in shape and are blue with tiny black dots except for the center of the top petal, which is white. Although the miniature lupine is small when compared with most lupines, its dense, conelike clusters make it conspicuous all the same.

Lupinus species have compound leaves of three to seventeen leaflets joined in a *palmate* (like fingers of a hand) arrangement. They have pealike pods that split open when dry, ejecting the seeds. The Fabaceae include many important food plants—peas, beans, peanuts, lentils, alfalfa, and clover—but lupines contain alkaloids that are poisonous to livestock and humans.

Janet Horton

SCIENTIFIC NAME	*Lupinus bicolor*
FAMILY	**Fabaceae** Legume
BLOOM	March–June

94 · Silver Bush Lupine

SCIENTIFIC NAME	*Lupinus albifrons* var. *albifrons*
FAMILY	**Fabaceae** Legume
BLOOM	March–June

Silver bush lupine, a perennial shrub, tolerates dry conditions and is common in chaparral, foothill woodlands, and sandy washes. To reduce moisture loss, it is covered in silky white hairs that give it the specific epithet *L. albifrons*, "white fronded."

The two lower petals of a lupine flower fit together to form a *keel* that encloses the male and female parts of the flower and *nectaries* where its nectar is stored. Only bees, which are heavy enough to force the petals of the keel apart, can reach the nectar. In doing so, they are also dusted with pollen and make contact with the stigma. Once a bush lupine flower has been pollinated, it stops producing nectar and the color of its banner patch changes from white to purple. Potential pollinators learn to avoid these dry flowers. Silver bush lupine is the host plant of the Boisduval's blue butterfly.

Larry Ulrich

95 · Vinegar Weed

Charles Rettner

SCIENTIFIC NAME	*Trichostema lanceolatum*
FAMILY	**Lamiaceae** Mint
BLOOM	August–October

Most humans find the scent of vinegar weed to be unpleasant, but it is an important nectar plant for bees as well as for sachem, woodland skipper, and umber skipper butterflies, and for the day-flying bumblebee clearwing moth. An annual, it blooms from late summer to fall in dry, open, generally disturbed areas.

The flowers occur in the axils where narrow leaves join its two-foot stem. They are fairly small—about 1/2 inch long or less—and dainty. The two upper petals are fused in the shape of a long, curved tube that arcs gracefully over a broad lower lip. Four long, thin stamens (*trichos*, "hair," plus *stema*, "stamens") protrude from this tube.

96 · Woolly Bluecurls

Woolly bluecurls is a woody perennial chaparral shrub that varies considerably in hue and in woolliness (*lanatum* means "woolly"), depending upon its location. It thrives after fires because it can regenerate from its root crown and also produces seeds that are stimulated to germinate by smoke.

The flower is similar to that of its annual cousin, vinegar weed, but made more colorful by the pink-and-blue wool covering its calyx as well as by its arrangement in dense clusters. The two-inch leaves of woolly bluecurls are considered pleasantly fragrant.

Keir Morse

SCIENTIFIC NAME	*Trichostema lanatum*
FAMILY	**Lamiaceae** Mint
BLOOM	May–August

Clusters of chia flowers encircle their four-sided stems at intervals, like deep blue ruffs above sharp-pointed bracts. The *scapose* (leafless) stems emerge from rosettes of leaves that are dark green with minute bristles and divided *pinnately* (divided like a feather).

Chia is a common annual plant in dry scrub, chaparral, and disturbed sites. It produces lots of seeds. Like a number of other dry habitat species, the seeds of chia have a coating that becomes mucilaginous when wet, helping them to remain moist long enough for the seeds to germinate and causing sand and soil to stick to them, hiding them from rodents. This mucilage has also made them a filling beverage for indigenous Californians during lean times.

Larry Ulrich

SCIENTIFIC NAME	*Salvia columbariae*
FAMILY	**Lamiaceae** Mint
BLOOM	March–June

Thistle sage is another common annual in chaparral and sandy or gravelly soils. It is a silvery plant, with woolly hairs that reflect sunlight and baffle dry breezes that would otherwise dry out its tissues. Like its unrelated namesake, thistle sage has a frilly rosette of prickly leaves at its base. Encircling its bare stem are one to four clusters of bright lavender flowers that each have long, sharp bracts spread out beneath them.

The inch-long blossoms have fringed, two-lipped corollas with two *exserted* (protruding) stamens. These stamens bear conspicuous orange anthers at their tips, which contrast colorfully with the purple flowers and silver foliage.

Larry Ulrich

SCIENTIFIC NAME	*Salvia carduacea*
FAMILY	**Lamiaceae** Mint
BLOOM	March–May

99 · Fringed Onion

Fringed onion is another flower with a frail, dainty appearance that seems inconsistent with the harsh conditions of one of its favored habitats: rock and scree. It is also common on dry slopes and flats. The challenges of its environment made it a much-dwarfed member of the lily family compared with blue dicks or brodea. It is a perennial with clusters of rose-purple flowers that have three petals and three sepals united in a funnel-shaped *perianth.*

Wild onions are edible, though the flavor can be so strong as to make them unpalatable. They are said to have been used by native Californians and early settlers to prevent scurvy.

Keir Morse

SCIENTIFIC NAME	*Allium fimbriatum* var. *fimbriatum*
FAMILY	**Liliaceae** Lily
BLOOM	March–July

100 · Chinese Houses

Charles Rettner

Chinese houses are much-anticipated annuals on shaded flats or on the slopes of oak woodlands. In some years there are millions in bloom; other years are disappointing not only to human flower enthusiasts, but also to the bees with which they are popular.

Each flower has an upright lilac or white upper lip that has maroon speckles and lines at its base. The throat of the flower is bristly, and the style and stamens are hidden by the folded middle lobe of the darker, drooping lower lip. When a pollinator lands on this convenient platform, its weight depresses the lip to expose the male and female parts as well as the nectar.

These flowers are named for their resemblance to Chinese temples and apartment houses built in cities like San Francisco and Sacramento during the nineteenth century, which were often multistoried with eaves and balconies around the outside of each floor.

SCIENTIFIC NAME	*Collinsia heterophylla*
FAMILY	**Scrophulariaceae** Figwort
BLOOM	March–May

CALIFORNIA BIOREGIONS

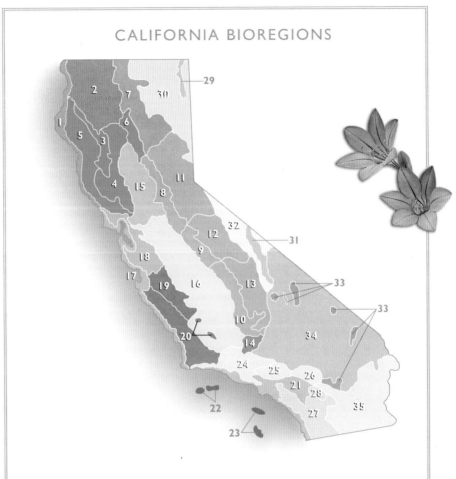

A bioregion is an area comprising a natural community that has a unique combination
of flora and fauna due to its climate, soils, hydrology, and other environmental conditions.

CALIFORNIA BIOREGIONS

1 North Coast
2 Klamath Ranges
3 High North Coast Ranges
4 Inner North Coast Ranges
5 Outer North Coast Ranges
6 Cascade Range Foothills
7 High Cascade Range
8 N Sierra Nevada Foothills
9 C Sierra Nevada Foothills
10 S Sierra Nevada Foothills
11 N High Sierra Nevada
12 C High Sierra Nevada
13 S High Sierra Nevada

14 Tehachapi Mountain Area
15 Sacramento Valley
16 San Joaquin Valley
17 Central Coast
18 San Francisco Bay Area
19 Inner South Coast Ranges
20 Outer South Coast Ranges
21 South Coast
22 N Channel Islands
23 S Channel Islands
24 Western Transverse Ranges
25 San Gabriel Mountains
26 San Bernardino Mountains

27 Peninsular Ranges
28 San Jacinto Mountains

GREAT BASIN BIOREGIONS

29 Warner Mountains
30 Modoc Plateau
31 White & Inyo Mountains
32 East of Sierra Nevada

DESERT BIOREGIONS

33 Desert Mountains
34 Mojave Desert
35 Sonoran Desert

PLANT DISTRIBUTION

1 White Globe Lily
Below 6,500 feet in the north and central Sierra Nevada
foothills, central western California, western Transverse
Ranges, northern Channel Islands.

2 Tooth Wort
Below 4,000 feet in the California Floristic Province,
Oregon, and Baja California.

3 Narrow-leaved Fringepod
Below 8,000 feet in the southern Sierra Nevada
foothills, Tehachapi Mountain area, San Francisco Bay
Area, South Coast Ranges, southwestern California, east
of Sierra Nevada, desert, and Baja California.

4 Jewelflower
Below 4,250 feet in the southern outer North Coast
Ranges, southernmost high North Coast Ranges, southern inner North Coast Ranges, San Francisco Bay Area,
northern outer South Coast Ranges, and northern and
central inner South Coast Ranges.

5 Evening Snow
Below 5,500 feet in the California Floristic Province,
White and Inyo mountains, desert, Arizona, and
Nevada.

6 Miner's Lettuce
Below 6,500 feet in the California Floristic Province,
Great Basin Floristic Province, Mojave Desert, Montana, and elsewhere in the west from British Columbia
to Montana.

7 California Saxifrage
Below 4,000 feet in the California Floristic Province,
southwest Oregon, and northwest Baja California.

8 Stinging Phacelia
Below 4,500 feet along the North Coast, in central
western California, and Oregon.

9 Popcornflower
Generally below 2,600 feet in the California Floristic
Province, rarely the edge of the desert, and from
Washington to Mexico.

10 Heliotrope
Below 7,000 feet in California, Nevada, Arizona,
and subtropical and tropical America.

11 California Man-root
Below 5,250 feet in the California Floristic Province except
for northern northwestern California and the northern
Cascade Range. Also found in the Mojave Desert.

12 Jimson Weed
Below 7,200 feet in the inner North Coast Ranges,
central and southern Sierra Nevada foothills, Tehachapi
Mountain area, Great Central Valley, central western
California, southwestern California, desert and in Utah,
Texas, and Mexico.

13 Silver Puffs
Below 5,900 feet throughout California except for the
North Coast, also in Oregon, Washington, Idaho,
Utah, western Texas, and northern Mexico.

14 Blow-wives
Below 3,000 feet in the California Floristic Province,
southern Oregon, and northern Baja California.

15 Wild Buckwheat
From 165 to 6,200 feet in central western California,
southwestern California, and Baja California.

16 California Buckwheat
Below 5,250 feet in central western California, southwestern California, and northwest Mexico.

17 Buck Brush
Below 5,900 feet in the California Floristic Province
except for the Great Central Valley.

18 Chamise
Below 5,250 feet in the southern North Coast Ranges,
Sierra Nevada, central western California, southwestern
California, and Baja California.

19 Narrow-leaf Milkweed
From 165 to 7,200 feet throughout California except
for the coastal areas. Also in Washington, Utah, and
Baja California.

20 Fremont's Death Camas
Below 3,280 feet in northwestern California, the
Sacramento Valley, central western California,
southwestern California, Oregon, and northern
Baja California.

21 Soap Plant
Below 5,000 feet in northwestern California, Sierra
Nevada foothills, the western Great Central Valley,
central western California, southwestern California, and
southwestern Oregon.

22 Black Sage
Below 4,000 feet in central western California, southwestern California, and northern Baja California.

23 Everlasting
Below 4,000 feet along the North Coast, outer North Coast Ranges, northern and central Sierra Nevada foothills, the Central Coast, San Francisco Bay Area, outer South Coast Ranges, South Coast, northern Channel Islands, San Bernardino Mountains, and Peninsular Ranges.

24 California Chicory
Below 6,560 feet in the southern North Coast, outer North Coast Ranges, central and southern Sierra Nevada foothills, Tehachapi Mountain area, Great Central Valley, central western California, southwestern California, southeast of the Sierra Nevada, the western Mojave Desert, Baja California.

25 California Plantain
Below 2,300 feet in the California Floristic Province, north to Oregon, and south to Baja California.

26 Desert Candle
From 500 to 5,000 feet in the southern Sierra Nevada foothills, the western edge of the central and southern San Joaquin Valley, the inner South Coast Ranges, northern western Transverse Ranges, and the southwestern Mojave Desert.

27 Douglas' Meadowfoam
Below 3,280 feet along the North Coast, in the North Coast Ranges, Cascade Range foothills, central Sierra Nevada foothills, Great Central Valley, Central Coast, San Francisco Bay Area, South Coast Ranges, and southwest Oregon.

28 Cream Cups
Below 3,280 feet in the California Floristic Province and western desert, as well as in Oregon, Utah, Arizona, and Baja California.

29 Pipestems
Below 6,560 feet in the Sierra Nevada foothills, central western California, and southwestern California.

30 Golden Eardrops
Below 5,900 feet in northwestern California, central western California, the Sierra Nevada, southwestern California, and northern Baja California.

31 Sun Cup
Below 5,000 feet in northwestern California, the Cascade Range, Sierra Nevada foothills, Great Central Valley, central western California, the Modoc Plateau, Washington, Idaho, and western Nevada.

32 Bush Poppy
Below 5,900 feet in southern northwestern California, the Cascade Range foothills, Sierra Nevada foothills, central western California, southwestern California, and northern Baja California.

33 California Buttercup
Below 7,900 feet in the California Floristic Province, southern Oregon, and Baja California.

34 Golden Yarrow
Below 10,000 feet in the North Coast Ranges, Sierra Nevada, central western California, southwestern California, western edge desert; also Baja California.

35 Goldenaster
Below 3,600 feet in the central and southern Sierra Nevada Foothills, Tehachapi Mountain area, San Joaquin Valley, central western California, South Coast, Transverse Ranges, and Peninsular Ranges.

36 Goldfields
Below 5,000 feet in the California Floristic Province and west Mojave Desert, as well as in southwest Oregon, Arizona, and Mexico.

37 Common Madia
Below 11,000 feet in the California Floristic Province (except the Channel Islands), the Great Basin Floristic Province, Oregon, and Baja California.

38 Munz's Tidytips
Below 2,300 feet in the San Joaquin Valley.

39 Three-rayed Tarweed
Below 2,300 feet in the Cascade Range foothills, eastern San Francisco Bay Area, and inner South Coast Ranges.

40 Shrubby Butterweed
Below 5,250 feet in the California Floristic Province except for the North Coast and Klamath Ranges, and in Baja California.

41 Gray Mule-ears
Below 6,560 feet in the southern North Coast Ranges, central Sierra Nevada foothills, and central western California.

42 Whispering Bells
Below 7,200 feet in the high North Coast Ranges, inner North Coast Ranges, central and southern Sierra Nevada, San Joaquin Valley, central western California, southwestern California, east of the Sierra Nevada, and desert.

43 Desert Dandelion
Below 5,600 feet in the San Joaquin Valley, central western California, southwestern California, Mojave Desert, and Mexico.

44 Yellow Pincushion
Below 5,250 feet in the North Coast Ranges, Sierra Nevada foothills, Tehachapi Mountain area, Great Central Valley, central western California, southwestern

California, the western edge of the desert, and northern Baja California.

45 Rancher's Fireweed
California to British Columbia, Idaho, and Arizona; naturalized in the central and eastern United States and in South America.

46 Honeysuckle
Below 6,000 feet in the northern high Sierra Nevada, Tehachapi Mountain area, central western California, and southwestern California.

47 Bladder Parsnip
From 160 to 5,000 feet in the California Floristic Province and desert, to British Columbia.

48 Sanicle
Below 3,280 feet in northwestern California, central western California, southwestern California, the Sierra Nevada foothills, and beyond British Columbia, Baja California, and southern South America.

49 Valley Tassels
Below 4,000 feet in the California Floristic Province and in British Columbia, northern Baja California, and central Chile.

50 Hoary Nettle
Below 10,000 feet in the California Floristic Province except northwestern California, the White and Inyo mountains, and desert mountains as well as elsewhere in the western United States and northern Mexico.

51 Deerweed
Below 5,000 feet on the North Coast, North Coast Ranges, northern Sierra Nevada foothills, Central Coast, San Francisco Bay Area, South Coast, western Transverse Ranges, Peninsular Ranges, and Baja California.

52 California False Lupine
Below 7,000 feet in northwestern California, Cascade Range, central western California, southwestern California, Modoc Plateau, and Oregon.

53 Common Monkeyflower
Below 8,200 feet, California to Alaska, western Canada, the Rocky Mountains, and northern Mexico.

54 Johnny Jump-up
Below 3,280 feet in the outer and inner North Coast Ranges, San Francisco Bay Area, central western California, southwestern California, and northern Baja California.

55 California Poppy
Below 6,560 feet in the California Floristic Province, just east of the Sierra Nevada, the Mojave Desert, to southern Washington, Nevada, New Mexico, and northwest Baja California.

56 Wind poppy
Below 4,000 feet in southern northwestern California, the southern Sierra Nevada foothills, San Joaquin Valley, central western California, southwestern California, and northern Baja California.

57 Western Wallflower
Below 13,000 feet in California, except for the Great Central Valley, and to the east-central United States.

58 Sticky Monkeyflower
Below 5,250 feet in the California Floristic Province and northwest edge of the Sonoran Desert.

59 Red Maids
Below 7,200 feet in the California Floristic Province, western Modoc Plateau, southeast of the Sierra Nevada, northern desert mountains and to New Mexico, Central America, and also in northwest South America.

60 California Catchfly
Below 7,200 feet in northwestern California, the Cascade Range, Sierra Nevada, Central Coast, San Francisco Bay Area, northern outer South Coast Ranges, western Transverse Ranges (northern slopes), and western San Gabriel Mountains.

61 Lance-leaved Dudleya
Between 100 and 4,100 feet in the South Coast Ranges, Transverse Ranges, Peninsular Ranges, desert mountains, and northern Baja California.

62 Venus Thistle
Below 11,800 feet in the California Floristic Province (except the San Joaquin Valley), the Modoc Plateau, White and Inyo mountains, and western Mojave Desert, to southern Oregon, southwest Idaho, and western Nevada.

63 Scarlet Bugler
Below 6,000 feet in the North Coast Ranges, northern Sierra Nevada foothills, Great Central Valley, central western California, southwestern California, southwest edge of the Mojave Desert, and Mexico.

64 California Figwort
Eastern northwestern California, southern Sierra Nevada, central western California, and the South Coast.

65 Indian Warrior
Below 7,000 feet in northwestern California, the Cascade Range, Sierra Nevada foothills, Tehachapi Mountain area, central western California, southwestern California, and southern Oregon.

66 Indian Paintbrush
Below 4,000 feet along the central North Coast, northern outer North Coast Ranges, southern outer North Coast Ranges, northern Cascade Range

foothills, Sierra Nevada foothills, central western California, southwestern California, and Baja California.

67 California Fuchsia
Below 5,000 feet in the California Floristic Province (except the high Sierra Nevada) and desert mountains.

68 Western Columbine
Below 11,000 feet in the California Floristic Province (except Great Central Valley, South Coast, Channel Islands), Great Basin Floristic Province, desert mountains, and north Alaska and Montana, south into Baja California.

69 Four-spot
Below 5,000 feet in the California Floristic Province and north to Washington as well as in Arizona and Baja California.

70 Elegant Clarkia
Below 5,000 feet in the North Coast Ranges, Sierra Nevada foothills, Tehachapi Mountain area, San Francisco Bay Area, South Coast Ranges, South Coast, western Transverse Ranges, and the Peninsular Ranges.

71 California Rose
Below 5,250 feet in the California Floristic Province except for the high Cascade Range and high Sierra Nevada, as well as in southern Oregon and northern Baja California.

72 Bitter Root
From above 200 and below 9,800 feet in the Klamath Ranges, high North Coast Ranges, inner North Coast Ranges, Sierra Nevada, San Francisco Bay Area, inner South Coast Ranges, Transverse Ranges, San Jacinto Mountains, Modoc Plateau, east of the Sierra Nevada, desert mountains (the Panamint Mountains, and to the Rocky Mountains.

73 Slender-flowered Gilia
Above 300 feet and below 4,600 feet in the Central Coast and South Coast Ranges.

74 Pink Spineflower
Below 5,250 feet in northwestern California, the Cascade Range, Sierra Nevada foothills, Tehachapi Mountain area, Great Central Valley, central western California, the northern western Transverse Ranges, and southern Oregon.

75 Pitcher Sage
Between 500 and 3,000 feet in the North Coast Ranges, Cascade Range foothills, northern and central Sierra Nevada foothills, San Francisco Bay Area, outer South Coast Ranges, and western Transverse Ranges.

76 Chaparral Pea
Below 2,200 feet in the North Coast Ranges, northern Sierra Nevada foothills, and San Francisco Bay Area; below

5,500 feet in southern areas including the South Coast Ranges, northern Channel Islands, and Transverse Ranges.

77 Pinpoint Clover
Below 6,000 feet in the California Floristic Province (except the Channel Islands) and the Mojave Desert and Washington and Arizona.

78 Purple Owl's-clover
Below 5,250 feet in northwestern California, the Sierra Nevada foothills, Great Central Valley, central western California, southwestern California, and the western Mojave Desert.

79 Baby Blue-eyes
Between 50 and 5,250 feet in the California Floristic Province and Mojave Desert.

80 Blue Fiesta Flower
Below 6,250 feet in the inner North Coast Ranges, southern Sierra Nevada, central Sierra Nevada foothills, Tehachapi Mountain area, San Joaquin Valley, central western California, southwestern California, and the northeast Sonoran Desert to Arizona.

81 Shooting Star
Below 2,000 feet in the northern and central Sierra Nevada foothills, central high Sierra Nevada, Great Central Valley, San Francisco Bay Area, and inner South Coast Ranges.

82 Blue Witch
Below 5,250 feet in northwestern California, the Great Central Valley delta areas, central western California, southwestern California, Arizona, and Baja California.

83 Blue-eyed Grass
Below 7,900 feet in California and Oregon.

84 Douglas Iris
Below 3,280 feet in northwestern California, central western California, northern southwestern California, and Oregon.

85 Ithuriel's Spear
Below 5,000 feet in northwestern California, the Cascade Range, Sierra Nevada, central western California, Transverse Ranges, and southwestern Oregon.

86 Elegant Brodiaea
Below 7,200 feet in the Klamath Ranges, northern and central North Coast Ranges, Sierra Nevada, San Francisco Bay Area, and southwest Oregon.

87 Blue Dicks
Below 7,500 feet from California to Oregon, Utah, New Mexico, and northern Mexico.

88 Many-flowered Eriastrum
Below 6,650 feet in central and southern Sierra Nevada

foothills, San Joaquin Valley, San Francisco Bay Area, eastern South Coast Ranges, and western Mojave Desert.

89 Lax Snapdragon
Below 4,300 feet in the southern outer North Coast Ranges, central western California, southwestern California, and northwestern Baja California.

90 Parry's Larkspur
Below 8,500 feet in the Tehachapi Mountain area, central western California, southwestern California, and northern Baja California.

91 Fleabane Daisy
Below 9,500 feet in the southern Sierra Nevada, outer South Coast Ranges, Transverse Ranges, Peninsular Ranges, desert mountains, and northern Baja California.

92 Houndstongue
Below 5,000 feet in northwestern California (except the high North Coast Ranges), Cascade Range, Sierra Nevada foothills, northern high Sierra Nevada, San Francisco Bay Area, South Coast Ranges, north to British Columbia.

93 Miniature Lupine
Below 5,250 feet in the California Floristic Province, north to British Columbia, south to Baja California, and naturalized in Arizona.

94 Silver Bush Lupine
Below 5,000 feet in the North Coast Ranges, Sierra Nevada foothills, central western California, and South Coast.

95 Vinegar Weed
Below 3,280 feet in the California Floristic Province, Oregon, and Baja California.

96 Woolly Bluecurls
Below 2,600 feet in the South Coast Ranges, South coast, western Transverse Ranges, San Gabriel Mountains, Peninsular Ranges, and Baja California.

97 Chia
Below 4,000 feet in California (except Klamath Ranges, Cascade Range, and northern Sierra Nevada) and into Utah and Arizona.

98 Thistle Sage
Below 4,600 feet in the Tehachapi Mountain area, San Joaquin Valley, eastern San Francisco Bay Area, inner South Coast Ranges, southwestern California, western desert, and northern Baja California.

99 Fringed Onion
Between 975 and 8,850 feet in the southern North Coast Ranges, southern Sierra Nevada foothills, Tehachapi Mountain area, central western California, southwestern California, desert, and northern Baja California.

100 Chinese Houses
Below 3,280 feet in the California Floristic Province and northern Baja California.

FURTHER READING

Casebeer, MaryRuth, *Discover California Wildflowers.* Sonora, Calif.: Hooker Press, 1998.

Hickman, James C., *Jepson Manual: Higher Plants of California.* Berkeley: The University of California Press, 1993.

Leigh, Carol *California Wildflower Locations,* Waldport, Ore.: Picture This, 2001 (A cd of species, their bloom dates, and locations where they may be found, available at http://www.photoexplorations.com/home.htm)

Munz, Philip A., *Introduction to California Spring Wildflowers of the Foothills, Valleys, and Coast* (Revised Edition). Berkeley: The University of California Press, 2004.

Niehaus, Theodore F. and Charles L. Ripper, *A Field Guide to Pacific States Wildflowers : Washington, Oregon, California and adjacent areas.* Boston: Houghton Mifflin, 1998.

INDEX